HMH SCIENCE DIMENSIONS™
CHEMISTRY

Module J

This Write-In Book belongs to

_____

Teacher/Room

_____

Houghton Mifflin Harcourt™

Consulting Authors

Michael A. DiSpezio

Global Educator
North Falmouth,
Massachusetts

Michael DiSpezio has authored many HMH instructional programs for Science and Mathematics. He has also authored numerous trade books and multimedia programs on various topics and hosted dozens of studio and location broadcasts for various organizations in the United States and worldwide. Most recently, he has been working with educators to provide strategies for implementing the Next Generation Science Standards, particularly the Science and Engineering Practices, Crosscutting Concepts, and the use of Evidence Notebooks. To all his projects, he brings his extensive background in science, his expertise in classroom teaching at the elementary, middle, and high school levels, and his deep experience in producing interactive and engaging instructional materials.

Marjorie Frank

Science Writer and Content-Area Reading Specialist
Brooklyn, New York

An educator and linguist by training, a writer and poet by nature, Marjorie Frank has authored and designed a generation of instructional materials in all subject areas, including past HMH Science programs. Her other credits include authoring science issues of an award-winning children's magazine, writing game-based digital assessments, developing blended learning materials for young children, and serving as instructional designer and coauthor of pioneering school-to-work software. In addition, she has served on the adjunct faculty of Hunter, Manhattan, and Brooklyn Colleges, teaching courses in science methods, literacy, and writing. For *HMH Science Dimensions™*, she has guided the development of our K–2 strands and our approach to making connections between NGSS and Common Core ELA/literacy standards.

Acknowledgments

Cover credits: (blue crystal formation) ©Houghton Mifflin Harcourt; (sodium acetate crystals in flask) ©Charles D. Winters/Science Source.

Section Header Master Art: (waves, computer artwork) ©Alfred Pasieka/Science Source

ISBN   978-0-544-86102-2

10 0877   25 24 23 22 21 20 19

4500745873   C D E F G

Michael R. Heithaus, PhD

Dean, College of Arts, Sciences & Education
Professor, Department of Biological Sciences
Florida International University
Miami, Florida

Mike Heithaus joined the FIU Biology Department in 2003 and has served as Director of the Marine Sciences Program and Executive Director of the School of Environment, Arts, and Society, which brings together the natural and social sciences and humanities to develop solutions to today's environmental challenges. He now serves as Dean of the College of Arts, Sciences & Education. His research focuses on predator-prey interactions and the ecological importance of large marine species. He has helped to guide the development of Life Science content in *HMH Science Dimensions™*, with a focus on strategies for teaching challenging content as well as the science and engineering practices of analyzing data and using computational thinking.

Cary I. Sneider, PhD

Associate Research Professor
Portland State University
Portland, Oregon

While studying astrophysics at Harvard, Cary Sneider volunteered to teach in an Upward Bound program and discovered his real calling as a science teacher. After teaching middle and high school science in Maine, California, Costa Rica, and Micronesia, he settled for nearly three decades at Lawrence Hall of Science in Berkeley, California, where he developed skills in curriculum development and teacher education. Over his career, Cary directed more than 20 federal, state, and foundation grant projects and was a writing team leader for the Next Generation Science Standards. He has been instrumental in ensuring *HMH Science Dimensions™* meets the high expectations of the NGSS and provides an effective three-dimensional learning experience for all students.

Program Advisors

Paul D. Asimow, PhD
Eleanor and John R. McMillan
Professor of Geology and
Geochemistry
California Institute of Technology
Pasadena, California

Joanne Bourgeois
Professor Emerita
Earth & Space Sciences
University of Washington
Seattle, WA

Dr. Eileen Cashman
Professor
Humboldt State University
Arcata, California

Elizabeth A. De Stasio, PhD
Raymond J. Herzog Professor of
Science
Lawrence University
Appleton, Wisconsin

Perry Donham, PhD
Lecturer
Boston University
Boston, Massachusetts

Shila Garg, PhD
Emerita Professor of Physics
Former Dean of Faculty & Provost
The College of Wooster
Wooster, Ohio

Tatiana A. Krivosheev, PhD
Professor of Physics
Clayton State University
Morrow, Georgia

Mark B. Moldwin, PhD
Professor of Space Sciences and
Engineering
University of Michigan
Ann Arbor, Michigan

Ross H. Nehm
Stony Brook University (SUNY)
Stony Brook, NY

Kelly Y. Neiles, PhD
Assistant Professor of Chemistry
St. Mary's College of Maryland
St. Mary's City, Maryland

John Nielsen-Gammon, PhD
Regents Professor
Department of Atmospheric
Sciences
Texas A&M University
College Station, Texas

Dr. Sten Odenwald
Astronomer
NASA Goddard Spaceflight Center
Greenbelt, Maryland

Bruce W. Schafer
Executive Director
Oregon Robotics Tournament &
Outreach Program
Beaverton, Oregon

Barry A. Van Deman
President and CEO
Museum of Life and Science
Durham, North Carolina

Kim Withers, PhD
Assistant Professor
Texas A&M University-Corpus
Christi
Corpus Christi, Texas

Adam D. Woods, PhD
Professor
California State University,
Fullerton
Fullerton, California

Classroom Reviewers

You are a scientist!
You are naturally curious.

Have you ever wondered . . .

- why is it difficult to catch a fly?
- how a new island can appear in an ocean?
- how to design a great tree house?
- how a spacecraft can send messages across the solar system?

HMH SCIENCE DIMENSIONS™

will *SPARK* your curiosity!

AND prepare you for

✓	tomorrow
✓	next year
✓	college or career
✓	life!

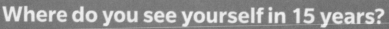

Where do you see yourself in 15 years?

Observe

Collect Data

Be a scientist.
Work like real scientists work.

Analyze

Be an engineer.
Solve problems like engineers do.

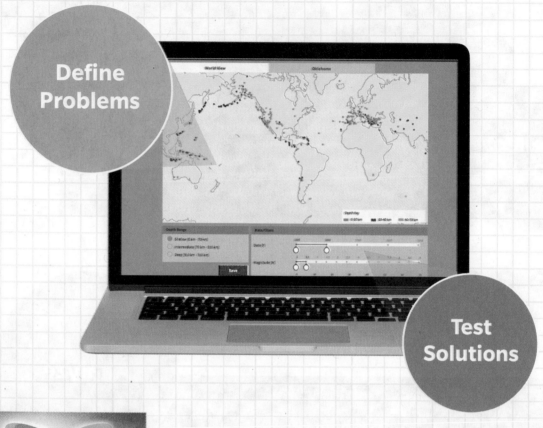

Define Problems

Test Solutions

STEM

Gather Information

Think Critically

Explain your world.
Start by asking questions.

Conduct Investigations

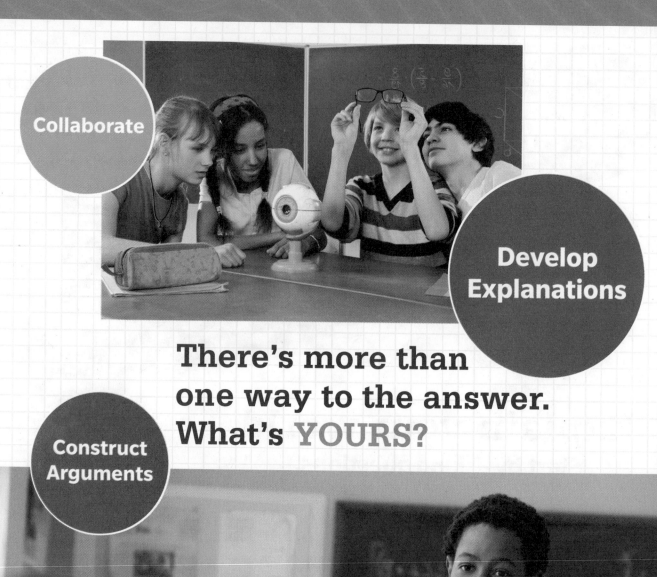

Collaborate

Develop Explanations

There's more than one way to the answer. What's YOURS?

Construct Arguments

YOUR Program

Write-In Book:

- a brand-new and innovative textbook that will guide you through your next generation curriculum, including your hands-on lab program

Interactive Online Student Edition:

- a complete online version of your textbook enriched with videos, interactivities, animations, simulations, and room to enter data, draw, and store your work

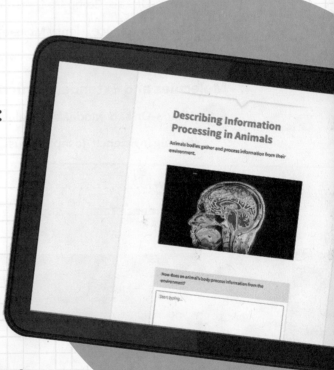

More tools are available online to help you practice and learn science, including:

- **Hands-On Labs**
- **Science and Engineering Practices Handbook**
- **Crosscutting Concepts Handbook**
- **English Language Arts Handbook**
- **Math Handbook**

UNIT 1

The Structure of Matter

Seashells are made mostly of calcium carbonate, a substance made up of calcium, carbon, and oxygen atoms.

UNIT 2

States of Matter and Changes of State

Solid water provides an icy home to these penguins.
They are also at home swimming in the liquid ocean water.

Contents

UNIT 3

Chemical Processes and Equations

Fireflies, also called lightning bugs, are small insects that generate their own light using chemical reactions.

UNIT 4 179

The Chemistry of Materials

The material that makes up these fabrics is ideal for clothing.
Fabric can be made with natural or synthetic materials.

Whether you are in the lab or in the field, you are responsible for your own safety and the safety of others. To fulfill these responsibilities and avoid accidents, be aware of the safety of your classmates as well as your own safety at all times. Take your lab work and fieldwork seriously, and behave appropriately. Elements of safety to keep in mind are shown below and on the following pages.

Safety in the Lab

- [ ] Be sure you understand the materials, your procedure, and the safety rules before you start an investigation in the lab.

- [ ] Know where to find and how to use fire extinguishers, eyewash stations, shower stations, and emergency power shutoffs.

- [ ] Use proper safety equipment. Always wear personal protective equipment, such as eye protection and gloves, when setting up labs, during labs, and when cleaning up.

- [ ] Do not begin until your teacher has told you to start. Follow directions.

- [ ] Keep the lab neat and uncluttered. Clean up when you are finished. Report all spills to your teacher immediately. Watch for slip/fall and trip/fall hazards.

- [ ] If you or another student are injured in any way, tell your teacher immediately, even if the injury seems minor.

- [ ] Do not take any food or drink into the lab. Never take any chemicals out of the lab.

Safety in the Field

- [ ] Be sure you understand the goal of your fieldwork and the proper way to carry out the investigation before you begin fieldwork.

- [ ] Use proper safety equipment and personal protective equipment, such as eye protection, that suits the terrain and the weather.

- [ ] Follow directions, including appropriate safety procedures as provided by your teacher.

- [ ] Do not approach or touch wild animals. Do not touch plants unless instructed by your teacher to do so. Leave natural areas as you found them.

- [ ] Stay with your group.

- [ ] Use proper accident procedures, and let your teacher know about a hazard in the environment or an accident immediately, even if the hazard or accident seems minor.

Safety Symbols

To highlight specific types of precautions, the following symbols are used throughout the lab program. Remember that no matter what safety symbols you see within each lab, all safety rules should be followed at all times.

Dress Code

- Wear safety goggles (or safety glasses as appropriate for the activity) at all times in the lab as directed. If chemicals get into your eye, flush your eyes immediately for a minimum of 15 minutes.
- Do not wear contact lenses in the lab.
- Do not look directly at the sun or any intense light source or laser.
- Wear appropriate protective non-latex gloves as directed.
- Wear an apron or lab coat at all times in the lab as directed.
- Tie back long hair, secure loose clothing, and remove loose jewelry. Remove acrylic nails when working with active flames.
- Do not wear open-toed shoes, sandals, or canvas shoes in the lab.

Glassware and Sharp Object Safety

- Do not use chipped or cracked glassware.
- Use heat-resistant glassware for heating or storing hot materials.
- Notify your teacher immediately if a piece of glass breaks.
- Use extreme care when handling any sharp or pointed instruments.
- Do not cut an object while holding the object unsupported in your hands. Place the object on a suitable cutting surface, and always cut in a direction away from your body.

Chemical Safety

- If a chemical gets on your skin, on your clothing, or in your eyes, rinse it immediately for a minimum of 15 minutes (using the shower, faucet, or eyewash station), and alert your teacher.
- Do not clean up spilled chemicals unless your teacher directs you to do so.
- Do not inhale any gas or vapor unless directed to do so by your teacher. If you are instructed to note the odor of a substance, wave the fumes toward your nose with your hand. This is called wafting. Never put your nose close to the source of the odor.
- Handle materials that emit vapors or gases in a well-ventilated area.
- Keep your hands away from your face while you are working on any activity.

Safety Symbols, continued

Electrical Safety

- Do not use equipment with frayed electrical cords or loose plugs.
- Do not use electrical equipment near water or when clothing or hands are wet.
- Hold the plug housing when you plug in or unplug equipment. Do not pull on the cord.
- Use only GFI-protected electrical receptacles.

Heating and Fire Safety

- Be aware of any source of flames, sparks, or heat (such as flames, heating coils, or hot plates) before working with any flammable substances.
- Know the location of the lab's fire extinguisher and fire-safety blankets.
- Know your school's fire-evacuation routes.
- If your clothing catches on fire, walk to the lab shower to put out the fire. Do not run.
- Never leave a hot plate unattended while it is turned on or while it is cooling.
- Use tongs or appropriately insulated holders when handling heated objects.
- Allow all equipment to cool before storing it.

Plant and Animal Safety

- Do not eat any part of a plant.
- Do not pick any wild plant unless your teacher instructs you to do so.
- Handle animals only as your teacher directs.
- Treat animals carefully and respectfully.
- Wash your hands throughly with soap and water after handling any plant or animal.

Cleanup

- Clean all work surfaces and protective equipment as directed by your teacher.
- Dispose of hazardous materials or sharp objects only as directed by your teacher.
- Wash your hands throughly with soap and water before you leave the lab or after any activity.

Student Safety Quiz

Circle the letter of the BEST answer.

1. Before starting an investigation or lab procedure, you should
   - **A.** try an experiment of your own
   - **B.** open all containers and packages
   - **C.** read all directions and make sure you understand them
   - **D.** handle all the equipment to become familiar with it

2. At the end of any activity you should
   - **A.** wash your hands thoroughly with soap and water before leaving the lab
   - **B.** cover your face with your hands
   - **C.** put on your safety goggles
   - **D.** leave hot plates switched on

3. If you get hurt or injured in any way, you should
   - **A.** tell your teacher immediately
   - **B.** find bandages or a first aid kit
   - **C.** go to your principal's office
   - **D.** get help after you finish the lab

4. If your glassware is chipped or broken, you should
   - **A.** use it only for solid materials
   - **B.** give it to your teacher for recycling or disposal
   - **C.** put it back into the storage cabinet
   - **D.** increase the damage so that it is obvious

5. If you have unused chemicals after finishing a procedure, you should
   - **A.** pour them down a sink or drain
   - **B.** mix them all together in a bucket
   - **C.** put them back into their original containers
   - **D.** dispose of them as directed by your teacher

6. If electrical equipment has a frayed cord, you should
   - **A.** unplug the equipment by pulling the cord
   - **B.** let the cord hang over the side of a counter or table
   - **C.** tell your teacher about the problem immediately
   - **D.** wrap tape around the cord to repair it

7. If you need to determine the odor of a chemical or a solution, you should
   - **A.** use your hand to bring fumes from the container to your nose
   - **B.** bring the container under your nose and inhale deeply
   - **C.** tell your teacher immediately
   - **D.** use odor-sensing equipment

8. When working with materials that might fly into the air and hurt someone's eye, you should wear
   - **A.** goggles
   - **B.** an apron
   - **C.** gloves
   - **D.** a hat

9. Before doing experiments involving a heat source, you should know the location of the
   - **A.** door
   - **B.** window
   - **C.** fire extinguisher
   - **D.** overhead lights

10. If you get chemicals in your eye you should
    - **A.** wash your hands immediately
    - **B.** put the lid back on the chemical container
    - **C.** wait to see if your eye becomes irritated
    - **D.** use the eyewash station right away, for a minimum of 15 minutes

Go online to view the Lab Safety Handbook for additional information.

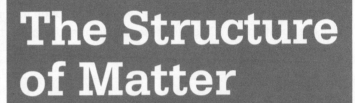

The Structure of Matter

This portion of the Eagle Nebula photographed by the Hubble Space Telescope is nicknamed the "Pillars of Creation." A nebula is a cloud of dust and gas in outer space. When the matter in a nebula gets very dense, new stars can form.

The universe is full of matter. Here on Earth, matter makes up everything from the air we breathe to the food we eat. What makes up matter? In this unit, you will explore models that represent the building blocks of matter. You also learn how the arrangement of these building blocks affects a substance's physical properties.

Why It Matters

Here are some questions to consider as you work through the unit. Can you answer any of the questions now? Revisit these questions at the end of the unit to apply what you discover.

Questions	Notes
Can you name some chemical elements you use or see on a regular basis?	
What would happen if you tried to cut a sheet of aluminum foil in half over and over again?	
Why does a 10-gram piece of copper take up more space than a 10-gram piece of gold?	
What do we mean when we say a substance is "pure"?	
Why do we fill balloons with helium gas instead of oxygen gas?	
How does the molecular structure of a material influence its physical properties?	

Unit Starter: Comparing Structure and Behavior

Beads and bricks are small units that can be combined to make larger objects. The arrangement of these units affects the properties of the objects in these photographs.

1. In each set of images, the object on the right is made up of
   the same / different materials as in the image on the left.

2. Which of the following statements are correct? Choose all that apply.

   A. A brick wall has more stability than a pile of bricks.

   B. Beads on a string are more tightly packed than beads in a jar.

   C. A brick wall follows a repeating pattern, while a pile of bricks is disorganized.

   D. A string of beads has a defined arrangement, but a jar of beads does not.

 Go online to download the Unit Project Worksheet to help you plan your project.

Unit Project

Simple or Complex?

Carbohydrates are important nutrients that fuel our bodies and give us the energy to work, play, and think. Nutritionists can tell you that not all carbohydrates are the same, though. Some are simple molecules, while others have more complex structures. Create models of simple and complex carbohydrates. Explain how their structures relate to their physical properties and their use by the human body.

The Properties of Matter

Some materials can glow on their own, without being supplied electricity. They have a property that makes them different from other materials.

By the end of this lesson . . .

you will be able to use the properties of matter to help explain the behavior of substances.

Go online to view the digital version of the Hands-On Lab for this lesson and to download additional lab resources.

CAN YOU EXPLAIN IT?

How can you tell the difference between the materials in these two rocks?

Miners must be able to tell substances apart from one another when they look for metal ores. These rocks may look similar, but they are made of different substances. The rock on the left contains large amounts of lead, and the rock on the right contains large amounts of iron.

1. Observe these two rocks. How do they appear similar? How do they appear different?

2. What do you think might explain these similarities and differences?

EVIDENCE NOTEBOOK As you explore the lesson, consider ways in which two similar-looking objects could be distinguished from one another.

Defining Matter

Think about everything around you during your day. The water you splash on your face, your shirt, the air blowing through your hair, and your desk at school all have something in common. They are all matter. *Matter* is a word used to describe physical things. Most things you can see or feel are matter, but some are not.

A basketball is made of matter.

Fire itself is not matter. However, the wood that burns is matter.

3. A basketball is very different from a fire. What are some differences that might make a basketball matter but not a fire?

Matter

All matter, including basketballs and water, shares two properties. **Matter** is anything that has mass and takes up space. Both living and nonliving things are matter. Your body, a tiny ant, and the rocks and soil in a garden are all matter. Some things that you cannot see are also matter. Air is matter. It takes up space inside a basketball. However, the actual flame that you see in a fire is a combination of light and heat. Neither light nor heat have mass or take up space. Because fire does not have mass or take up space, fire is not matter.

4. Which of the following would be considered matter? Choose all that apply.

   A. light from the sun

   B. milk in a carton

   C. heat from a candle

   D. sound of booming thunder

   E. pebble on a beach

Everything that takes up space and has mass is matter. Even the air, which you cannot see, is matter.

Mass

Ants and humans are made up of very different amounts of matter. **Mass** is a measure of the amount of matter in an object. Objects made up of more matter have a greater mass. You have more mass than an ant because you contain more matter. Mass depends only on the amount of matter in an object. It does not depend on the shape of object. The mass of an object does not necessarily depend on its size, either. For example, a beach ball has less mass than a bowling ball, even though the beach ball is larger.

The photo shows mass being measured using a scale. A scale, or balance, measures mass in units of grams (g). Large masses are often measured in kilograms (kg). Very small masses are often measured in milligrams (mg).

5. What do the readings on the digital scales indicate about the two pieces of clay?

Two pieces of clay have been molded into two different shapes. The mass of clay can be measured using a scale, such as those shown here.

Weight

When you pick up an object to judge how heavy it is, you are not actually measuring how much matter is in the object. What you are feeling is the object's weight. **Weight** is a measure of the gravitational force on an object. The gravitational force keeps objects on Earth from floating into space. Scientists measure weight using the unit newtons (N). Weight is also commonly measured in pounds (lb).

The greater the mass of an object, the greater the gravitational force on the object. Therefore, the more mass an object has, the greater the object's weight is. For example, the two pieces of clay from the photo have the same weight on Earth because they have the same mass. However, weight also depends on gravity. The strength of the gravitational force affects the weight. Gravity is greater on Jupiter than on Earth, because Jupiter has more mass than Earth. Therefore, the clay pieces would weigh more on Jupiter. But their masses would be the same on Jupiter as they are on Earth. The only way to change an object's mass is to add or remove matter.

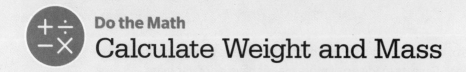

Do the Math

Calculate Weight and Mass

Many scales are designed to measure weight, not mass. Even though these scales do not directly measure mass, the mass of an object can be easily calculated from the object's weight. Weight is a force that depends on the acceleration due to gravity and the mass of an object. If you know how strong gravity is and can measure the weight of an object, you can calculate the mass of the object.

The following equation shows the relationship between mass (m), force (F), and acceleration (a). This equation can be used to calculate the mass of an object if you know the weight, which is a force, and the acceleration due to gravity:

$$m = \frac{F}{a}$$

The mass of the object is represented by the variable m. You solve the equation to find this variable.

The weight of an object is a force, represented by the variable F. Force is measured in newtons or $kg \cdot m/s^2$.

The variable a is acceleration. Acceleration related to an object's weight is the result of gravity, which is 9.8 m/s² on Earth.

6. Calculate the mass of the bag of glass based on the weight (F) shown. The measurement from the scale is given in the caption.

$$m = \frac{F}{a}$$

$$m = \frac{\boxed{} \; kg \cdot m/s^2}{9.8 \; m/s^2}$$

$m = $ _____ kg

Scales that use units of newtons or pounds measure weight, not mass. This scale shows gravity's pull on the bag of glass exerting a force, or weight, of 4.9 N on the scale.

You can also rearrange the equation to calculate the weight if you know the mass:

$$F = m \times a$$

7. Calculate the weight of the rocks in the photo.

$F = m \times a$

$F = $ _____ kg × 9.8 m/s²

$F = $ _____ kg · m/s²

Scales that measure mass typically use units of grams or kilograms. This scale shows that the mass of these rocks is 0.5 kg.

8. Can a substance be identified by only its mass or weight? Record your evidence.

Explain Weight on the Moon

When astronauts landed on the moon, they could carry very heavy pieces of equipment. They could also jump much farther than they could on Earth. They did all of this while wearing a spacesuit that weighed about 180 lb on Earth. Wearing the spacesuit on Earth would be like carrying around another person. Astronauts train for their missions to space, but they do not have superhuman strength. The astronauts' abilities on the moon are related to the mass of the moon, which is much smaller than the mass of Earth.

On the moon, astronauts can carry objects that would be too heavy to carry on Earth.

9. Acceleration due to gravity on the moon is greater / less than acceleration due to gravity on Earth. The mass of an object on the moon is less than / greater than / the same as it is on Earth. Using the equation $F = ma$ to calculate weight, the mass of an object is multiplied / divided by acceleration due to gravity. So, the weight of an object on the moon is greater / less than the weight of the same object on Earth.

Measuring Volume and Density

Someone else cannot sit in the seat you are sitting in at the same time. You take up the space in the seat. All matter takes up space, even matter you cannot see. Gases, such as helium or air, fill up the space inside balloons like the ones in the photo.

10. The gas inside each balloon takes up the same amount of space. The difference in the mass of the balloons is only a few grams at most. The balloon resting on the table is filled with air. The floating balloon is filled with helium gas. Why might the helium balloon float while the other rests on the table?

    A. Helium has less mass in the same amount of space than air does, so the helium balloon sinks in air.

    B. Helium has less mass in the same amount of space than air does, so the helium balloon floats in air.

    C. Air has less mass in the same amount of space than does helium, so the helium balloon sinks in air.

    D. Air has less mass in the same amount of space than helium does, so the helium balloon floats in air.

Helium gas is taking up space inside the floating balloon. Air is taking up space inside the other balloon.

Volume

You may describe the size of an object by calling it *big* or *small*. You can also measure its volume. **Volume** is a measure of the amount of space an object takes up. It is the three-dimensional size of the object, which is why the units for volume are cubic centimeters (cm^3) or cubic meters (m^3). The volume of liquids and gases can also be measured in milliliters (mL) or liters (L). One milliliter equals one cubic centimeter.

Volume can be measured in several different ways. The volume of a gas, such as air, is always the same as the volume of the container that the gas is in. The volume of a liquid, like water, is measured with tools such as graduated cylinders or beakers. The volume of a solid is measured in different ways depending on the shape of the object.

Measure Volume with a Formula

You can calculate the volume of regular-shaped objects using measurements. Regular-shaped objects include a rectangular box (prism), a spherical ball, or a cylindrical tube. To find the volume of a rectangular prism, you measure the length, width, and height of the prism. Then, you multiply those measurements using the formula:

$$V = \textit{length} \times \textit{width} \times \textit{height}$$

11. Find the volume of this box using the formula for a rectangular prism.

$V = length \times width \times height$

$V = $ _____ cm $\times$ _____ cm $\times$ _____ cm

$V = $ _____ cm^3

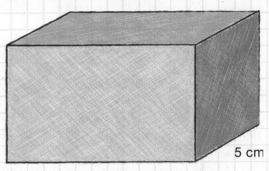

6 cm

5 cm

10 cm

Measure Volume Using Displacement

Many objects, such as a rock or a fork, have irregular shapes. Their length, height, or width depends on what part of the object you measure. You cannot use a simple formula to calculate the volume of these objects. Instead, you can measure the volume of liquid that is displaced by the object. This method, called *displacement*, works because two pieces of matter cannot be in the same space. When an object is placed in water, the water is moved out of the way, or displaced. The volume of the water that is displaced equals the volume of the object that is underwater.

This rock has an irregular shape. The volume of water in the beaker is 300 mL.

12. Find the volume of the rock in the images by the amount of water that it displaces.

Initial volume of water = _____ mL

Volume of water with object = _____ mL

Volume of object = volume of displaced water =

Volume of water with object − initial volume of water =

_____ mL − _____ mL = _____ mL or cm^3

The rock is completely underwater. The volume of the water and the rock is now 450 mL.

Density

The volume and mass of a given material can change. Pouring out half a glass of water decreases the volume and mass by half. However, the density of the water does not change. **Density** is the ratio of the mass of a substance to its volume. The more mass in a given volume, the greater the density of the object. For example, the air-filled balloon has a greater density than the helium-filled balloon. The air-filled balloon has more matter in the same amount of space. You can calculate the density (*D*) of an object by dividing its mass (*m*) by its volume (*V*):

$$D = \frac{m}{V}$$

The units for density are the units for mass divided by the units for volume. For liquids, the units for density are grams per milliliter (g/mL). For solids, the units for density are grams per cubic centimeter (g/cm^3) or kilograms per cubic meter (kg/m^3).

Hands-On Lab
Measure Density

You will measure the mass and volume of objects in order to calculate their density. You will use formulas as well as the water displacement method to measure the volume of these objects.

A book and a brick are regular-shaped objects whose dimensions can be measured with a meterstick. The volume of irregular-shaped objects, such as a large key, should be measured using water displacement.

MATERIALS
- graduated cylinder
- objects to be measured
- ruler (or meterstick)
- scale (or balance)
- water

Procedure

STEP 1 Select three objects for which you will calculate the density. Two of the objects can be any size, but should be rectangular prisms. The other object can be any shape, but must be solid metal and fit in a graduated cylinder. Record your objects in the first column of the table.

STEP 2 Predict which objects will be the most and least dense. Explain your reasoning.

STEP 3 Measure the mass of each object. Record your data in the table.

STEP 4 Measure the length, height, and width of the two rectangular prisms. Use these measurements to calculate the volumes of the two objects. Record your data in the table.

STEP 5 Calculate the density of each rectangular prism. Record your data in the table.

STEP 6 Use the water displacement method to determine the volume of the metal object. Make sure the object is completely underwater when you record its volume. Record your data in the table. Wipe up any spilled water immediately.

STEP 7 Calculate the density of the metal object. Record your data in the table.

Object	Volume	Mass	Density

Analysis

STEP 8 How are the masses and volumes of the objects related to their densities?

STEP 9 Which of the objects that you measured was the least dense?

STEP 10 Why did the least dense object you measured have such a low density?

EVIDENCE NOTEBOOK

13. Think about the two rocks shown at the beginning of this lesson. How do you think their densities might differ? Record your evidence.

Relate Density to Volume

An object's mass cannot change without adding or removing matter from the object. But heating or cooling a material can change its volume. For example, if you freeze water in an ice cube tray, you will notice that the ice takes up more room than the liquid water did.

14. What happens to the density of an object when the volume of that object increases and the mass remains the same? Explain your answer.

_____

_____

_____

_____

Identifying the Properties of Matter

Suppose you are playing a guessing game. You need to describe an object so someone can guess its identity. You might describe its size or weight, but the person guessing would likely need to know other properties of the object to guess what it is.

15. Discuss Identify three differences between the objects that you can see in the photo.

Notice how light reflects differently from the rock and the bell. *Luster* is a property that describes how light reflects and interacts with a substance.

States of Matter

One property that you might use to describe an object is its state of matter. Most of the matter around you is a solid, liquid, or gas. Ice, rocks, and the fabric of your shirt are all solids. They have definite shapes and volumes. Water that flows out of the sink and olive oil are both liquids. They take the shape of their container, but they have a definite volume. Helium and air are gases. They take the shape and volume of their containers.

The state of a substance can change. For example, liquid water freezes into ice and boils into water vapor. Certain properties of the water change, but other properties stay the same in any state. Changing the state of a substance does not change its identity.

16. Write the following state of matter under the photo that shows that state:
solid, liquid, gas

_____

_____

_____

17. In the photo, the juice is shown in its solid state and in its liquid state. What appears to have changed about the juice when it changed state?

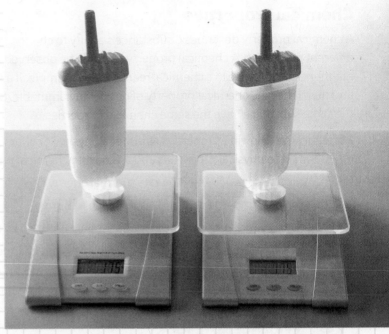

The juice on the left is a solid. It is a liquid on the right.

Properties of Matter

Matter has many properties that you can observe and measure. Some properties, such as mass and volume, depend on the amount of a material. Other properties, such as density, are the same for any amount of a material. Liquid water in a glass has the same density as a drop of water on the side of the glass. Density is a characteristic property that depends on the material. It can be used to help you identify a material. Properties can also be divided into physical properties and chemical properties.

Physical Properties

Mass, volume, density, and state are physical properties. A physical property is a property that can be observed without changing the identity of the substance. You can describe some physical properties just by looking at an object, including shape, color, and size. You can describe the texture by feeling an object. Some physical properties are also characteristic to a material. For instance, pieces of pure copper can all have different masses, but they will all melt at the same temperature.

18. Which of the following are requirements for something to be a physical property? Choose all that apply.

  A. The property can be observed without changing the identity of the substance.

  B. The property depends on the amount of the substance present.

  C. The state of the substance changes when you measure the property.

  D. The property can be observed or measured.

EVIDENCE NOTEBOOK

> **19.** How do the physical properties of the rocks at the beginning of the lesson differ? Are there physical properties that might differ, but that you cannot observe in the photos? Record your evidence.

Chemical Properties

A chemical property describes a substance's ability to change into a new substance with different properties. A chemical property can only be observed by trying to change the identity of a substance in a chemical reaction. For example, if a sample does not burn in a fire, then it has the chemical property of not being flammable. Small or large amounts of the same substance have the same chemical properties.

20. Label the following properties as either a physical or chemical property. Write a P next to physical properties and a C next to chemical properties.

    A. thermal conductivity—the rate thermal energy spreads through a substance _____

    B. flammability—the ability of a substance to burn _____

    C. magnetic attraction—whether a substance is pulled by a magnet _____

    D. melting point—the temperature at which a solid changes to a liquid _____

    E. reactivity with oxygen—the ability of a substance to chemically react with oxygen _____

 EVIDENCE NOTEBOOK

21. Do you think the rocks from the beginning of the lesson have different chemical properties? How could you test this? Record your evidence.

 22. **Language SmArts** On a separate sheet of paper, make a graphic organizer to show the relationships among physical properties, chemical properties, and properties that depend on the amount of a substance present.

 Engineer It
Recommend Materials for a Design Problem

Thermal conductivity is a physical property that describes how quickly a substance warms or cools. A substance with high thermal conductivity changes temperature quickly. A substance with low thermal conductivity changes temperature slowly. Suppose you are designing a refrigerator using the materials in the table.

Material	Thermal conductivity	Price
aluminum	high	expensive
plastic	low	inexpensive
aerogel	extremely low	very expensive

23. The walls of your refrigerator must keep as much heat as possible from getting inside the refrigerator. The refrigerator will use a lot of this material, so the cost must be low. Which material would you use to make the refrigerator's inner walls? Why?

    _____

    _____

24. The refrigerator needs a thermometer to respond quickly to temperature changes and keep the food inside cold. The thermometer is small, so it can be made out of pricier materials. Which material would you use to make the thermometer? Why?

    _____

    _____

Continue Your Exploration

Name: _____   **Date:** _____

Check out the path below or go online to choose one of the other paths shown.

Applications of Density

- **Hands-On Labs** ✋
- **Exploring Properties of Matter**
- **Propose Your Own Path**

Go online to choose one of these other paths.

Density is important in the natural world because it determines an object's ability to sink or float. It is the reason that ice covers the tops of lakes and that giant icebergs float in the ocean. Some fish control their density by changing the amounts of gases in their bodies so that they sink or float. Density is also important for technology. The bodies of airplanes are made from low-density materials to help them fly.

Huge, massive icebergs float in water instead of sinking.

1. Even though the iceberg and the water that surrounds it are made up of the same substance, the iceberg is able to float. Why is this?

   A. The volume of the iceberg equals the volume of an equal mass of water.

   B. The mass of the iceberg is greater than the mass of an equal volume of water.

   C. The volume of the iceberg is greater than the volume of an equal mass of water.

Continue Your Exploration

2. A submarine is able to raise and lower itself underwater. A rock sinks when it is dropped in a pool because it is denser than water. A piece of wood floats in the pool because it is less dense than water. What could the submarine change in order to sink or float? Choose all that apply.

   A. the submarine's volume

   B. the submarine's mass

   C. the state of the surrounding water

   D. the mass of the surrounding water

Submarines must be able to sink, rise, and stay at a certain depth in water.

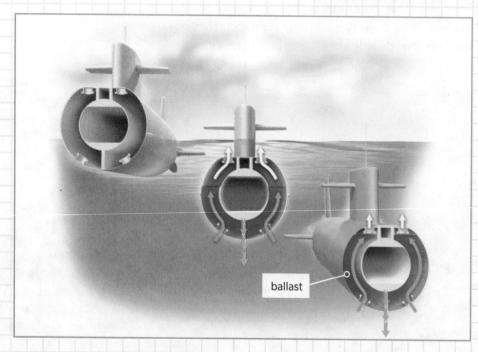

ballast

A submarine ballast enables the submarine to change its depth in the water.

3. A submarine fills a special storage area known as a *ballast* with water in order to increase its density. This allows it to dive deeper in the ocean. When a submarine needs to rise rapidly, compressed air is used to push the water out of the ballast. What effect does replacing the water in the ballast with air have on the submarine?

   A. The submarine's volume increases, lowering its density.

   B. The submarine's mass decreases, lowering its density.

   C. The submarine's mass increases, raising its density.

   D. The submarine's volume decreases, decreasing its density.

4. **Collaborate** With a partner, make a brochure that highlights an example of a technology that you have seen in which density is important.

Can You Explain It?

Name: _____   Date: _____

> **How can you tell the difference between the materials in these two rocks?**
>
>

EVIDENCE NOTEBOOK

Refer to the notes in your Evidence Notebook to help you construct an explanation for how you can tell the rocks apart.

1. State your claim. Make sure your claim fully explains how you can distinguish between materials that appear similar.

2. Summarize the evidence you have gathered to support your claim and explain your reasoning.

Checkpoints

Answer the following questions to check your understanding of the lesson.

Use the photo to answer Question 3.

3. Flammability is the ability of a substance to burn.

   The wood *has / does not have* this property.

   The metal pot *has / does not have* this property.

   This is a chemical property because the identity of the substances *changes / stays the same.*

4. The mass of a length of metal wire is 45 g. When the wire is placed in a graduated cylinder with water, it displaces 5 mL of water. What is the density of the metal?

   A. 0.1 g/cm^3

   B. 9 g/cm^3

   C. 40 g/cm^3

   D. 225 g/cm^3

Use the photo to answer Questions 5 and 6.

5. The photo shows mercury. Which of the following are physical properties of mercury that you can observe in the photo? Select all that apply.

   A. Its density is similar to the density of water.

   B. It is in the liquid state.

   C. It is shiny and gray.

   D. It is not attracted to magnets.

   E. It is able to react with oxygen.

6. Old thermometers contained very small amounts of mercury. The mercury in the photo has a melting point of −38.8 °C. What can you conclude about the melting point of the mercury in old thermometers?

   A. Its melting point can only be determined when the mercury is burned.

   B. Its melting point changes as the mercury's temperature changes.

   C. Its melting point equals −38.8 °C because it is mercury.

   D. Its melting point is less than −38.8 °C because its volume is smaller.

Interactive Review

Complete this page to review the main concepts of the lesson.

All matter has mass and takes up space. Mass is a measure of the amount of matter in an object or substance. Weight depends on both mass and gravity.

A. Compare and contrast mass and weight.

Volume is a measure of the amount of space an object takes up. Density is the ratio of mass to volume and thus does not depend on the amount of a substance.

B. Describe how you find the density of a substance.

Physical and chemical properties are used to describe and identify matter. Physical properties can be observed without changing the identity of a substance. Chemical properties can be observed by attempting to change the identity of a substance.

C. What are two physical and two chemical properties that you can use to help you identify a substance?

Atoms and Elements

The color of these lights depends on which element is inside the tubes.

By the end of this lesson . . .

you will be able to explain the relationship between atoms and elements.

Go online to view the digital version of the Hands-On Lab for this lesson and to download additional lab resources.

CAN YOU EXPLAIN IT?

Why do silver and copper have similar properties?

These two objects were manufactured using different materials. One bowl is made of copper and the other is made of silver. The two bowls are different colors, but copper and silver also have many properties in common.

1. What are some physical properties that the two bowls seem to share?

2. Why might copper and silver have similar properties even though they are different materials?

EVIDENCE NOTEBOOK As you explore the lesson, gather evidence to help explain how objects made of different materials can have similar properties.

Explaining Elements

Think about the materials that you see every day. Most materials can be separated physically into their parts. For instance, you can filter minerals out of water or melt rocks in order to separate metals from the rock.

A pure substance is a material that cannot be physically separated into its parts. Every pure substance has its own specific properties. Pure water always has the same set of properties. Many pure substances can also be separated into components, but only by chemically changing the substance.

Smelting is a process that uses heat to separate pure metals from a mixture that also contains other substances.

3. Do you think that every substance can be separated physically or chemically into other substances? Explain your answer.

Elements

Even though water cannot be physically separated, running electricity through water can break the water down into oxygen and hydrogen. Chemical processes such as this can break down many pure substances into their components. However, some pure substances cannot be separated physically or chemically. An **element** is a substance that cannot be separated or broken down into simpler substances by chemical means. Elements are the building blocks of all other substances. Both oxygen and hydrogen are elements. Currently, 118 elements are known. Most objects that you see are made up of combinations of these elements. For instance, a person contains large amounts of oxygen, hydrogen, and carbon. On the other hand, a diamond is made of pure carbon.

Hands-On Lab
Compare Densities

You will use density to identify which objects are made of copper. You will measure the mass and volume of several objects. You will then calculate the density of each object and use these densities to identify whether the objects could be pure copper.

One of the properties of an element is its density. Copper is a common metal used in electrical wiring, jewelry, and many household objects. Every object made of pure copper has the same density as other pure copper objects have. You can sometimes identify copper based on properties such as color, but other substances or mixtures might share these properties. While an element cannot be identified by its density alone, knowing the density of an object can give you one piece of evidence about its composition.

Procedure and Analysis

STEP 1 Use the balance or scale to measure the mass of the copper object. Record your data in the table.

STEP 2 Pour water into the graduated cylinder until the cylinder is about half full. Measure the volume of water in the cylinder. Record your data in the table.

STEP 3 Carefully place the copper object in the water so that it is fully submerged. Measure the volume of the object and the water in the cylinder. Record your data in the table.

STEP 4 Calculate the volume of the object by subtracting the volume of the water from the volume of the object and water. Record your data in the table.

STEP 5 Repeat Steps 1 through 4 using each of the additional objects and the stack of pennies.

Object	Mass (g)	Volume of object and water (mL)	Volume of water (mL)	Volume of object (mL)

STEP 6 Calculate the density of each of the objects you tested by dividing the mass of each object by the volume of that object. Record the densities in the table. For each of the objects you test, indicate whether it is likely that the object is pure copper. The density of pure copper is 8.93 g/mL. Remember that experimental results can vary somewhat from the reference value.

Object Identification		
Object	Density (g/mL)	Pure copper?

STEP 7 Pennies made after 1982 are made primarily of one element coated with a thin layer of copper that gives it the appearance of pure copper. Use the evidence from your experimental results and the table of densities to identify which element might make up most of a penny.

Density of Pure Substances	
Element	**Density**
aluminum	2.70
iron	7.85
nickel	8.91
zinc	7.14

STEP 8 Which of the objects that you tested seemed like it could be made of pure copper? Explain your answer using evidence.

Properties of Elements

Each element has a unique set of physical and chemical properties. For example, oxygen is very different from copper. Carbon is very different from either oxygen or copper. Some elements may have similar colors or similar densities, or they may react in similar ways. Copper and silver can both be used to make bowls because they have similar properties—they can be hammered into thin sheets. However, no two elements have exactly the same set of properties.

EVIDENCE NOTEBOOK

4. Could the two bowls you saw in the pictures earlier in this lesson be made of two different elements? How could you identify the two different elements? Record your evidence.

5. An element cannot be broken down into other substances by chemical or physical means. But you can still split a sample of an element into smaller pieces. For example, a piece of aluminum foil can be cut in half and then in half again, and all of the pieces will still be aluminum. What do you think will eventually happen if you could continue dividing that piece of aluminum foil?

Atoms

Although an element cannot be broken down into other substances, a sample of the element can be divided into smaller pieces. An **atom** is the smallest unit of an element that has the chemical identity of that element. Atoms of the same elements have the same chemical properties and behave similarly. Iron atoms found on a meteorite will behave the same way as an iron atoms pulled up from the bottom of the ocean.

Each element has its own chemical and physical properties due to the properties of its atoms. Each object that you see is made up of a huge number of atoms. Atoms are so tiny that they cannot be seen with an optical microscope. Even our most advanced microscopes can barely make out individual atoms.

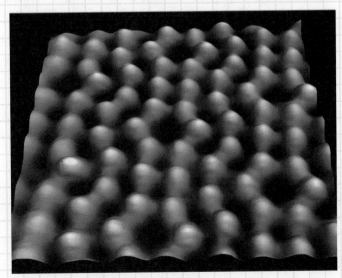

This image shows individual atoms on the surface of a piece of silicon. The image was made using a scanning tunneling microscope.

Do the Math | Model the Scale of an Atom Atoms are very tiny objects. It is difficult to imagine how small they are, so people use models to describe atoms. The largest atoms measure less than one nanometer in diameter. A nanometer is one one-billionth of a meter. If matter were expanded so that an atom could barely be seen, your body would be big enough to reach from Philadelphia, Pennsylvania, to Miami, Florida.

6. Each iron atom has a mass of about 9×10^{-23} grams. Even a small grain of iron has an incredible number of atoms in it—about 1×10^{18} atoms in one grain. Which of these is most similar to the number of atoms in a grain of iron?

   A. the number of people in a large stadium; about 1×10^5

   B. the number of people on Earth; about 1×10^{10}

   C. the number of meters between Earth and the star Vega; about 2.4×10^{17}

One of the tiny grains of iron shown has a mass of about 0.9 mg, or 9×10^{-4} grams.

7. This stadium can hold 100,000, or 1×10^5, people. The number of atoms in a grain of iron is about 1×10^{18}. Would you need 1×10^{10} or 1×10^{13} stadiums to hold the same number of people as the number of atoms in a grain of iron? Explain your answer.

Model Atoms and Elements

This ring has two different materials in it, gold and the diamond. Gold is an element. Diamonds are made of carbon, which is also an element.

8. **Draw** Make a sketch of the ring. Use patterns or colors to label which parts of the ring are composed of which types of atoms.

Analyzing the Properties of Elements

No two elements share the exact same set of properties. However, elements can still be similar to one another. Lead and carbon are both dark-colored elements. Germanium and silicon both can both be used to make semiconductors. Gold and platinum are both metals that are very stable because they react very slowly with other materials.

9. Look at a list of the elements or a periodic table. Identify some pairs of elements that you have heard of that have similar properties.

Many elements share properties. These are samples of carbon, silicon, germanium, tin, and lead. All of these samples are different elements, but they are similar in color.

Similarities between Elements

Since the first elements were identified, people have observed similarities among them. For example, gold and silver are both shiny metals that are easy to form into a shape or draw into a wire. Iron and copper are both metals that can be mixed with other substances to make strong, hard tools, such as knife blades and axes. Sodium and potassium are both soft metals that react vigorously with water and air. Once people knew about enough elements to observe patterns in their properties, they began to look for ways to organize this information. Scientists began to chart how the elements relate to one another. Each element has a huge number of properties. Finding a way to organize important information about each of the elements has taken years.

Language SmArts
Organize Items by Properties

When more and more elements were being discovered, scientists started looking for ways to organize lists of elements. Eventually, scientists started to organize the elements into charts using their properties. To understand the advantages and difficulties in using this type of chart, try organizing the balls listed into a chart.

10. Write the name of each type of ball in a space on the table. Place each item so the balls that are hollow or are in one column and those that are solid are in the other column. Place each item so that the mass increases as you go from left to right and top to bottom.

- bowling ball
- baseball
- ping pong ball
- basketball
- golf ball
- tennis ball

Hollow	Solid

The Periodic Table

Every element has a characteristic called its *atomic number*. The atomic number is based on the structure of the atoms that make up that element. Hydrogen is the smallest element, and has an atomic number of 1. The highest atomic number of the known elements is 118. The **periodic table** is an arrangement of all the known elements in order of their atomic number. Hydrogen is located at the top left corner of the table. The next element, helium, has the atomic number 2 and is at the top right corner of the table. In each row, or period, of the table, the atomic number increases from left to right.

The periodic table also organizes the elements based on their properties. Each column of the table, from top to bottom, includes elements that have similar physical and chemical properties. The elements in a column are called a *group*. The first column of the table, for example, contains a group of very reactive metal elements. The last column of the table contains a group of nonreactive elements that are all gases at room temperature. The elements in a group are similar but not identical to one another.

Representing Elements

The atomic number of an element is based on the structure of its atoms. The atomic number is related to the structure that determines the identity of the element, so each element has a different atomic number. Each box in the periodic table includes the atomic number of the element, the atomic mass of the element, which is also related to its structure, and the element's name and symbol.

For many of the symbols, it is obvious why they were chosen. For example, hydrogen (H), helium (He), and boron (B) have symbols directly related to their name. Other symbols are less obvious. Consider gold (Au), silver (Ag), and lead (Pb). These three elements have symbols derived from their Latin names: *aurum*, *argentum*, and *plumbum*.

Carbon in the Periodic Table

In order to understand the periodic table, you must understand how elements are represented in the table. Each element is listed in its own box with several pieces of information that can be quickly referenced.

6

C

Carbon

12.01

Atomic Number The atomic number is related to the structure of the atoms. Each element has a unique atomic number.

Atomic Symbol Every element is represented by a symbol of one, two, or three letters.

Atomic Name Some element names have been used for many centuries. Others are named after a person or place.

Atomic Mass All atoms have mass. The atomic mass of an element relates the mass of its atoms to the mass of a hydrogen atom.

11. Chemists use the periodic table to organize the elements. What are some ways in which this organization is useful? Select all that apply.

A. It groups elements that have similar properties.

B. It identifies which elements are most common and which are rare.

C. It allows scientists to predict how a particular element will interact with others.

D. It arranges elements in order of usefulness for human activities.

The Periodic Table of the Elements

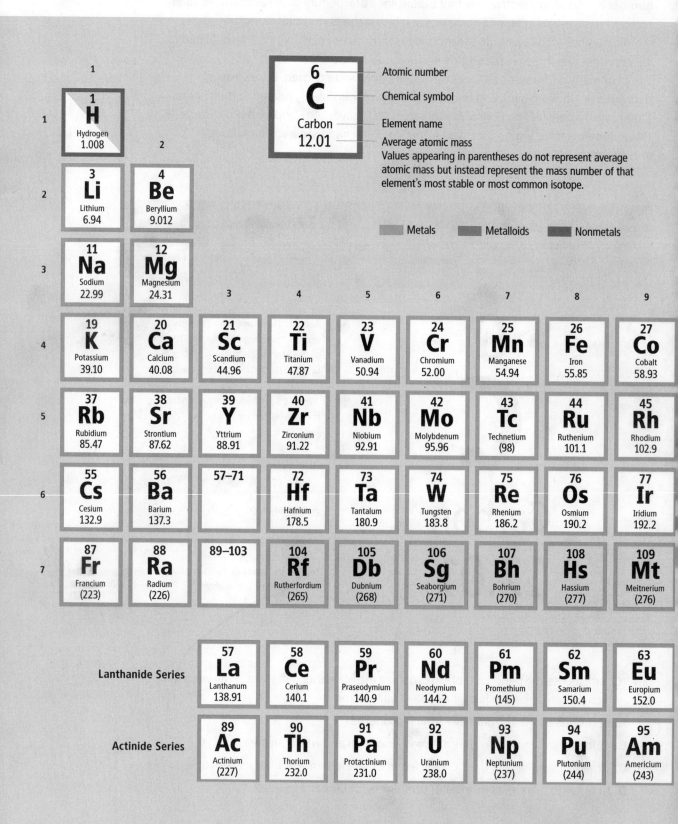

| | 6 C Carbon 12.01 | Atomic number |
| Chemical symbol |
| Element name |
| Average atomic mass |

Values appearing in parentheses do not represent average atomic mass but instead represent the mass number of that element's most stable or most common isotope.

Metals   Metalloids   Nonmetals

State of Element at STP

☐ Solid	◨ Liquid
◸ Gas	☐ Not yet known

Elements with atomic numbers of 95 and above are not known to occur naturally, even in trace amounts. They have only been synthesized in the lab. The physical and chemical properties of elements with atomic numbers 100 and above cannot be predicted with certainty.

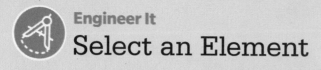

Engineer It
Select an Element

When choosing a material to use for an application, the properties of the material need to be taken into account. The periodic table provides a way to see how an element's properties relate to other elements. By using the periodic table, you can quickly see which elements fit engineering criteria.

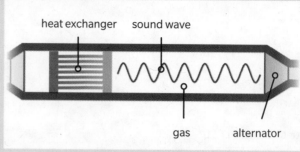

heat exchanger   sound wave

gas   alternator

A thermoacoustic generator uses sound waves in a gas to convert heat into electricity.

12. A thermoacoustic generator transforms thermal energy into electrical energy. Thermal energy is transferred to a gas by a heat exchanger. The thermal energy causes the gas particles to vibrate rapidly and generate a sound wave. These vibrating gas particles are then used by an alternator to generate electrical energy. The gas used in this kind of generator must be nonreactive to avoid the danger of fire. Using heavier gases increases the amount of electrical energy generated. Which two elements on the table are most likely to be good choices for use as the gas in a thermoacoustic generator?

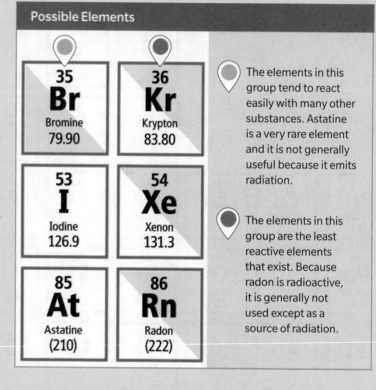

Possible Elements

35	36
Br	Kr
Bromine	Krypton
79.90	83.80

53	54
I	Xe
Iodine	Xenon
126.9	131.3

85	86
At	Rn
Astatine	Xenon
(210)	(222)

The elements in this group tend to react easily with many other substances. Astatine is a very rare element and it is not generally useful because it emits radiation.

The elements in this group are the least reactive elements that exist. Because radon is radioactive, it is generally not used except as a source of radiation.

_____

_____

_____

_____

_____

13. Explain how you can determine which gas is most likely to work well in a thermoacoustic generator based on position on the periodic table.

_____

_____

_____

_____

_____

 EVIDENCE NOTEBOOK

14. The materials that were used to make the bowls are similar in many ways. What might this tell you about the relationship between the two elements? Record your evidence.

Continue Your Exploration

Name: _____ **Date:** _____

Check out the path below or go online to choose one of the other paths shown.

People in Science

- Hands-On Labs
- Exploring Uses of Elements
- Propose Your Own Path

Go online to choose one of these other paths.

Henry Moseley, Physicist

Henry Moseley was a British physicist in the early part of the 20th century. Early in his career, he did research on the recently discovered radioactive element radium. During his research, he developed the first atomic battery. Atomic batteries are now used in medical devices and spacecraft. Moseley then began working on elements and the periodic table. Unfortunately, he died in combat during World War I when he was only 27 years old.

1. Early periodic tables organized elements based on their atomic masses and their properties. Why might this not be the best way to organize a periodic table? Select all that apply.

   A. Two elements might have similar atomic masses.

   B. Some elements are not very reactive.

   C. Using different properties could lead to a different grouping.

   D. Some elements do not have any properties.

Henry Moseley built his own equipment to prove that every element has its own x-ray frequency pattern.

Patterns and X-rays

When atoms gain a lot of energy, they can release x-rays. Henry Moseley shot high-energy particles at samples of elements to energize the samples. He discovered that each element would then emit an x-ray pattern specific to that element. Moseley found that these x-rays followed a pattern. The x-ray pattern that each element emitted corresponded to a whole number. These whole numbers are now known as the atomic numbers of elements. In general, these atomic numbers increased as the atomic masses increased, but there were some variations. When the periodic table was arranged using atomic numbers instead of atomic mass, some inconsistencies of earlier periodic tables disappeared.

Continue Your Exploration

Some inconsistencies in the periodic table disappeared when it was arranged using atomic numbers instead of atomic mass. Nickel and cobalt had posed problems in early periodic tables. The two elements had very similar atomic masses, which made determining their order difficult. However, the two elements have different atomic numbers, which allowed for them to be arranged consistently in periodic tables.

Mn 55.0	Fe 56, Ni 58.7, Co 59
Br 80.0	—
—	Ru 102, Rh 103, Pd 106

This is a portion of an early periodic table developed by Dmitri Mendeleev in 1898. He arranged elements by their atomic mass and properties.

24 **Cr** Chromium 52.00	25 **Mn** Manganese 54.94	26 **Fe** Iron 55.85	27 **Co** Cobalt 58.93	28 **Ni** Nickel 58.69
42 **Mo** Molybdenum 95.96	43 **Tc** Technetium (98)	44 **Ru** Ruthenium 101.1	45 **Rh** Rhodium 102.9	46 **Pd** Palladium 106.4

This is a portion of the modern periodic table that shows many of the same elements. These elements are arranged by their atomic number and their properties.

2. Moseley used his new version of the periodic table to predict four elements that had not previously been discovered. How might have using atomic numbers allowed Moseley to predict the existence of these four elements?

   A. Adding energy could change a known element into an unknown element.

   B. Gaps in the whole number pattern of atomic numbers might indicate undiscovered elements.

   C. There has to be an element that corresponds to every possible x-ray pattern.

   D. Discovery of unexpected x-ray patterns indicate additional elements are in a sample.

3. How might the atomic numbers of elements indicate that newly discovered elements would have to have very high atomic numbers?

4. **Collaborate** Discuss how factors other than the atomic number might affect the structure of the periodic table.

Can You Explain It?

Name: _____ Date: _____

Why do silver and copper have similar properties?

EVIDENCE NOTEBOOK

Refer to the notes in your Evidence Notebook to help you construct an explanation of how two different materials can have similar properties.

1. State your claim. Make sure your claim fully explains how two different materials can have similar properties.

2. Summarize the evidence you have gathered to support your claim and explain your reasoning.

Getty Images; (r) ©dontree_m/istock/Getty Images Plus/Getty Images

Checkpoints

Answer the following questions to check your understanding of the lesson.

Use the image to answer Question 3.

3. Which pair of elements is most likely to have similar properties?

   A. tungsten and osmium

   B. osmium and hassium

   C. seaborgium and rhenium

   D. bohrium and tungsten

74 **W** Tungsten 183.8	75 **Re** Rhenium 186.2	76 **Os** Osmium 190.2
106 **Sg** Seaborgium (271)	107 **Bh** Bohrium (270)	108 **Hs** Hassium (277)

4. Which properties do atoms of the same element share? Select all that apply.

   A. atomic number

   B. chemical reactivity

   C. melting point

Use the photos to answer Question 5.

5. The three elements in the photos all belong to the same group, or column, of the periodic table. These elements all produce salts when they react with metals. What are some differences between these elements?

   A. their colors

   B. their atomic masses

   C. the state of matter of each element

6. Imagine that you have a sample of a substance. You cannot physically separate that substance into components. You also cannot chemically separate that substance into components. Which of the following are true about your sample? Choose all that apply.

   A. The sample is made up of one type of atom.

   B. The sample is made up of multiple elements.

   C. The sample is made up of a single element.

   D. The sample is made up of several types of atoms.

Interactive Review

Complete this section to review the main concepts of the lesson.

Each element has its own chemical and physical properties due to the properties of its atoms.

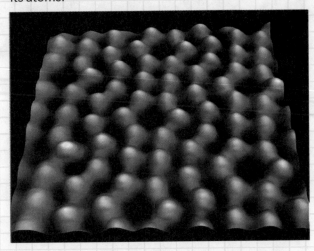

A. Explain the relationship between elements and atoms.

The periodic table is used to organize elements based on their properties. Elements in the same group have similar, but not identical, properties.

6
C
Carbon
12.01

B. What are some of the reasons that organizing elements in a periodic table is useful to scientists and engineers? Explain your answer.

Molecules and Extended Structures

Seashells are made mostly of calcium carbonate, a substance made up of calcium, carbon, and oxygen atoms.

By the end of this lesson . . .

you will be able to describe and model ways atoms can combine to make a variety of substances.

Go online to view the digital version of the Hands-On Lab for this lesson and to download additional lab resources.

CAN YOU EXPLAIN IT?

How can both of these samples be pure phosphorus?

These two samples are both pure phosphorus, made up of only phosphorus atoms. White phosphorus is a material used in some explosives and is considered to be unstable. In contrast, red phosphorus is considered to be more stable. It is a material used in match heads.

1. What are some differences you can observe in the two samples of phosphorus?

2. What explanation can you suggest for how two substances that look so different can both be made entirely of the same kind of atom?

 EVIDENCE NOTEBOOK As you explore the lesson, gather evidence to help explain how the two samples can both be pure phosphorus.

Describing the Composition of Matter

A **pure substance** is a sample of matter that has specific chemical and physical properties, such as appearance, melting point, and reactivity. Pure substances are made up of only one type of matter throughout. For any amount of pure substance you have, it will always be made of the same matter. For example, water is a pure substance. Whether you have a drop of water or a bathtub full of water, water always has the same properties because it is a pure substance.

The particles in pure substances can be groups of individual atoms that are not joined together, such as in helium gas, or they can be atoms that are joined together in different ways.

3. The particle structure of three pure substances are modeled below. Observe the arrangement of the atoms. Record your observations in the table.

Pure substance	Particle structure	Observations
chlorine	Cl Cl	
hydrogen	H H	
hydrogen chloride	H Cl	

4. Based on your observations, what is the same about **the three** models? What is different about the three models?

Atoms and Molecules

Atoms can be thought of as the building blocks of matter. An atom is the smallest unit of an element that keeps the properties of that element. Atoms joined in different ways make different substances. For example, chlorine and hydrogen atoms can be connected in different ways to make hydrogen, or chlorine, or hydrogen chloride.

5. Which of these models show atoms that have joined together? Explain.

A

B

C

A **molecule** is two or more atoms held together by chemical bonds. A **chemical bond** is the attractive force that holds atoms together. For example, an oxygen molecule contains two oxygen atoms connected by a chemical bond. Molecules can range in size from two atoms to thousands of atoms. The wide variety of matter that we see around us is a result of all the ways different atoms can combine.

Molecule of Oxygen

Oxygen is a molecule made up of two oxygen atoms.

Compounds

In some molecules, such as an oxygen molecule, all the atoms are the same type of atom. This type of molecule is an element. Elements are pure substances made entirely of the same type of atom.

In other molecules, such as a water molecule, there are two or more different types of atoms. These molecules form a type of matter called a compound. A **compound** is a pure substance made up of two or more different types of atoms joined by chemical bonds. A molecule is the smallest part of a compound that keeps the properties of that compound.

Compounds can be broken down into simpler substances. And compounds always form in a fixed ratio. For example, water always has two hydrogen atoms for every one oxygen atom. Water is a molecule because each particle of water is made up of two or more atoms held together by bonds. Water is also a compound because the water particle is made up of more than one type of atom, specifically hydrogen and oxygen.

6. Circle the molecules that are also compounds.

A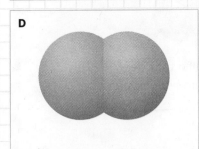

B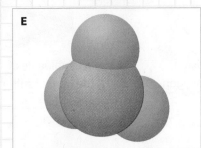

C

D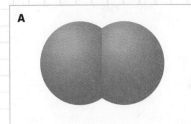

E

F

7. Which statements are true about molecules and compounds? Circle all that apply.

A. Molecules are made of one atom and compounds are made of two or more atoms.

B. Both molecules and compounds are pure substances.

C. The particles that make up compounds are molecules.

D. Hydrogen chloride is both a molecule and a compound.

 EVIDENCE NOTEBOOK

8. Both white phosphorus and red phosphorus are made up only of phosphorus atoms. Does this mean they are both pure substances? Could they be compounds? Record your evidence.

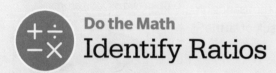
Do the Math
Identify Ratios

9. Each molecule of a substance is exactly the same. The atoms that make up the substance always combine in a fixed ratio. A ratio tells how much of one thing there is compared to another. When describing molecules, a ratio tells how much of one element there is compared to another element in the same molecule. For example, a molecule of water has 2 hydrogen atoms for every 1 oxygen atom. In other words, its ratio of hydrogen atoms to oxygen atoms is 2 to 1. Other ways to write the ratio are 2:1 and $\frac{2}{1}$.

For the statements below, write the correct ratio for the molecules described.

○ sulfur
● oxygen
● nitrogen

 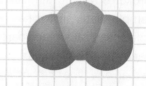

A. For every molecule of sulfur dioxide, the ratio of sulfur atoms to oxygen atoms is 1: _____.

B. In a molecule of nitrogen dioxide, the ratio of nitrogen atoms to oxygen atoms is _____ : 2.

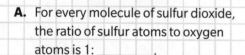 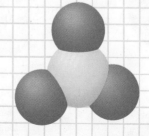

C. For every molecule of nitrous oxide, the ratio of nitrogen atoms to oxygen atoms is: $\frac{\quad}{1}$.

D. In a molecule of sulfur trioxide, the ratio of sulfur atoms to oxygen atoms is _____ : _____.

10. **Draw** A sodium atom joined with a chlorine atom forms the compound sodium chloride. Sodium chloride has properties that are different from the properties of sodium or chlorine alone. In a similar way, a compound word is the joining together of two different words. The word *dog* joined with the word *house* forms the compound word *doghouse*. The word *doghouse* has a different meaning compared to the meanings of the words *dog* or *house* alone.

Write two more compound words that are formed by the joining of two words. Use either *dog* or *house* as part of one of your new words. Then draw a picture to show the meaning of your two new compound words.

sodium atom + chlorine atom = sodium chloride

dog   +   house   =   doghouse

Word 1	Word 2	Compound Word	Drawing

Compare Models of Elements and Compounds

The diagrams show models of three different pure substances: water, table salt, and tin metal.

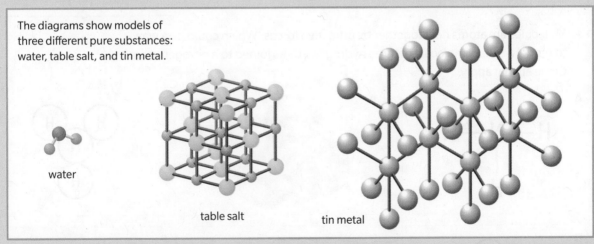

water

table salt

tin metal

11. Water, table salt, and tin metal are all pure substances. Which of these pure substances are compounds? Explain your reasoning.

_____

_____

_____

_____

Analyzing the Structure of Matter

Molecules are extremely small. A water molecule, for instance, is about 3 × 10⁻¹⁰ m (0.0000000003 m) in diameter, which is very much smaller than the period at the end of this sentence. The structure of matter at the atomic and molecular levels is too small to observe directly. So what do scientists do when they want to study these structures? They develop and use models of atoms and molecules. Scientists use models to help them understand the real world and how it works. Models can help us learn about and visualize things we cannot see directly.

12. There are many different types of models. The images at the right show some different ways to model molecules. How are the models alike? How are they different?

Examples of Molecular Models

These examples show three molecules modeled in different ways.

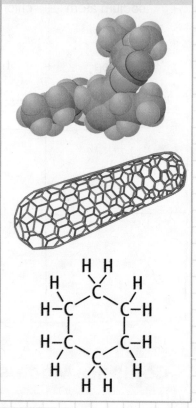

13. Molecules are atoms held together by attractive forces. Which could be a way to model a simple molecule of three hydrogen atoms joined to a nitrogen atom? Circle all that apply.

A
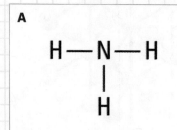

B
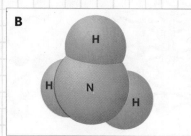

C
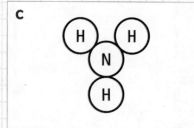

D
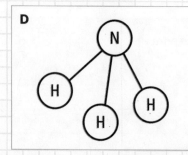

E
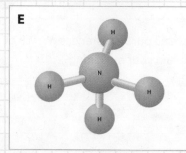

F
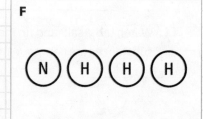

Models of Simple Molecules

There are many different ways to model molecules. A model of the simplest molecule would show just two atoms joined together. The atoms could be the same, such as in hydrogen, which has two hydrogen atoms. Or the atoms could be different, such as in a molecule of carbon monoxide, which is made up of one carbon atom and one oxygen atom. Other models could show three or more atoms.

Molecules are atoms joined together by chemical bonds. In some models you may see the chemical bonds represented by lines or sticks. But a chemical bond is not a physical thing. It is the attractive force that holds atoms together. Some models do not show anything at all to represent chemical bonds. They may instead show two atoms—perhaps, two spheres—that touch each other.

Two Types of Molecular Models

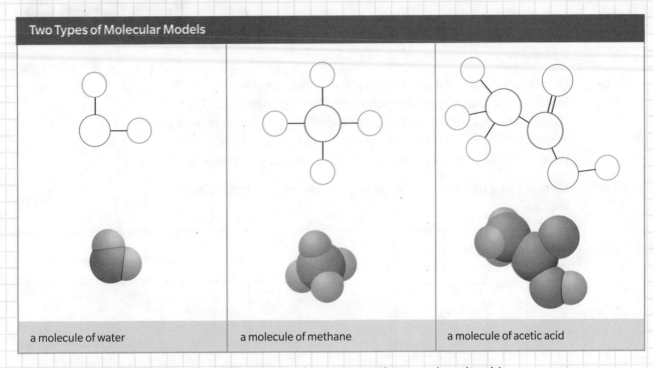

| a molecule of water | a molecule of methane | a molecule of acetic acid |

14. The diagrams above show two different ways that water, methane, and acetic acid can be modeled. Look closely at each type of model. Explain what each type of model shows best.

Hands-On Lab
Model Molecules

You will observe two compounds that are made of only carbon, hydrogen, and oxygen atoms. You will plan and carry out an investigation to explore how models of each molecule can explain why the compounds are different.

MATERIALS
• clay
• sample of acetic acid
• sample of isopropyl alcohol
• toothpicks

Procedure

STEP 1 Look at the samples of acetic acid and isopropyl alcohol. What properties can you observe? Record your observations in the table below.

STEP 2 On a separate piece of paper, make a plan to build a model of each molecule. Use the structural formulas from the table to help you. Think about how you can use the materials provided by your teacher to build the models. What can you make with the clay to represent part of the models? What can the toothpicks represent? Write the steps of your plan.

STEP 3 Carry out your plan for building the models. Then draw what you built in the table.

Compound Name	Molecule Structure	Observations	Draw Your Model
Acetic Acid	H—C—C with O and O—H (acetic acid structure)		
Isopropyl Alcohol	H—C—C—C—H with H, O, H below and H at bottom (isopropyl alcohol structure)		

Analysis

STEP 4 How are the structures of acetic acid and isopropyl alcohol similar? How are they different?

STEP 5 Why do you think acetic acid and isopropyl alcohol have different properties? Use the models you developed to help you explain.

Models of Complex Molecules

A simple molecule may contain a few atoms bonded together. A complex molecule may contain thousands of atoms. The atoms in complex molecules often form a repeating pattern. A repeating unit can be formed by a single type of atom or two or more different types of atoms. There is much variety. Most of the molecules of life are made up of complex molecules based around carbon. Complex molecules like these are possible because carbon atoms are able to form very stable bonds with each other.

Some plastics, such as the plastic in these chairs, contain thousands of carbon, hydrogen, and chlorine atoms joined together in long chains.

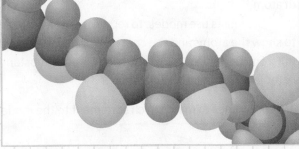

This model shows how a molecule of the plastic polyvinyl chloride (PVC) is made up of repeating units of carbon, hydrogen, and chlorine atoms.

15. This model is another way to show the structure of a molecule of PVC. Circle the unit that repeats.

$$
\begin{array}{cccccc}
H & H & H & H & H & H \\
| & | & | & | & | & | \\
-C- & C- & C- & C- & C- & C- \\
| & | & | & | & | & | \\
H & Cl & H & Cl & H & Cl
\end{array}
$$

16. Observe the diamond photo and its molecular structure diagram. Describe the repeating unit in the structure.

The Structure of the Diamond Substance

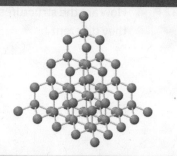

You may be familiar with diamonds as a precious gemstone. It is also one of the hardest natural materials on Earth. Diamond can be used to cut through other very hard materials, such as rock.

Diamond is a pure carbon substance. There is a repeating structure in a diamond, even though the atoms are all the same.

Extended Structures

A particle of matter is a pure substance in its simplest form. Particles of a pure substance can be atoms or molecules. In many solids, these particles are arranged in a very specific, repeating order. A substance in which the particles are arranged in an orderly, geometric, and repeating pattern is called a **crystal**. Crystals are solids that form by a regular repeated pattern of particles connecting together. The unit is repeated in the same arrangement over and over throughout the entire pure substance.

These extended structures are different from molecules and can be compounds or elements. For example, table salt has an extended structure that is made up of two types of atoms, sodium and chlorine. A model of table salt shows the repeating pattern of these atoms. Silver also has an extended structure, but it is composed of just one type of atom.

Scientists use models to represent molecules and extended structures, with parts to show the atoms and the chemical bonds that join them. Atoms can combine in many different ways to form a wide variety of pure substances. Models help you visualize the complex arrangements of atoms.

17. Draw lines to match each statement to the model it describes.

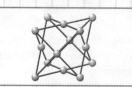

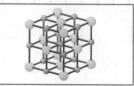

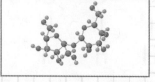

Table sugar is a molecule made up of carbon, hydrogen, and oxygen atoms arranged as two rings joined together.

Silver metal is an extended structure made up of atoms of silver arranged in a regular pattern.

Table salt is an extended structure made up of sodium and chlorine atoms arranged in a repeating pattern.

Evaluate Molecule Models

Deoxyribonucleic acid (DNA) is a molecule found in all living things that contains genetic information. DNA is a *macromolecule*, or large molecule, that is made up of many smaller molecules.

You have been given two models to help you analyze the structure of DNA.

- The model on the left looks something like a curved ladder. The blue "ribbon" represents a sugar-phosphate backbone of smaller molecules that forms the structure of the DNA. Each of the four colored "bars" represents a different type of smaller molecule. This model shows how the smaller molecules are connected within the DNA macromolecule.

- The model on the right also shows the overall spiral structure of DNA, but shows the individual atoms rather than showing types of molecules.

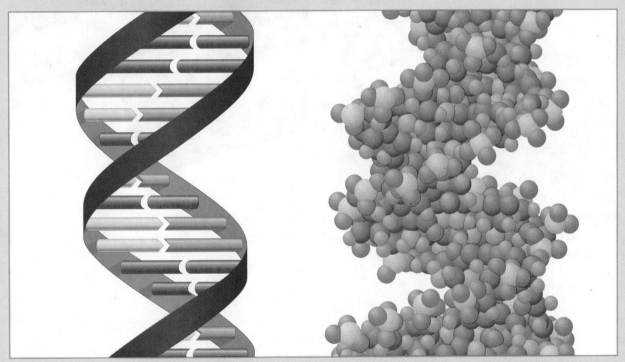

Both models show a section of DNA. The models use color to distinguish the various parts of the structure of DNA, but they show the DNA differently. The model on the left shows how smaller molecules within the DNA macromolecule are connected. The model on the right shows individual atoms.

---

18. If you are interested in finding patterns in the way the smaller molecules bond to make up DNA, which model would be most helpful? Complete the explanation.

The model on the left / right shows the atoms that make up the smaller molecules. It shows the detailed shape of the entire section of DNA, but not all the molecules are clearly seen. The model on the left / right shows how smaller molecules within the DNA are bonded to each other. It shows the order and relative position of the smaller molecules and the general shape of the DNA.

The model on the left / right is best for finding patterns in the way the smaller molecules bond.

Relating the Identity and Structure of Matter to Its Properties

Properties of Pure Substances

Why is a beam of iron so hard? Why is table sugar white and granular? Why does any substance have the properties it has? Structures at the atomic and molecular levels are too small for us to see, but it is important that we understand what is happening at these levels. The properties of a substance that we observe depend on the atoms that make up the substance and on the way those atoms are connected to each other.

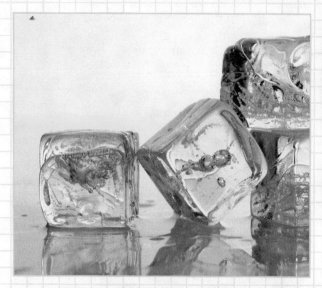 

19. Suppose you have a sample of two pure substances: a solid piece of ice and a solid piece of copper metal. Which would be easier to break apart? Explain your reasoning.

20. What might explain the differences in properties of the two pure substances: ice and copper metal? Circle all that apply.

   A. The substances differ in the types of atoms they contain and how they are connected.

   B. The chemical bonds that hold the atoms together may be stronger in one substance than in the other.

   C. There's a difference in the structure of the two substances.

   D. Copper metal is stronger than all other substances, including ice.

Relate Atom Type to Properties

Look at the objects in each row of the table. Even though the objects are formed from substances made of completely different atoms, the substances have similar properties because the atoms themselves have similar properties. The objects are made up of atoms from the same group of elements in the periodic table.

Similar Atoms Have Similar Properties

Group 11 Elements The properties of metals in this group, such as gold, silver, and copper, make them popular to use in jewelry. They are shiny and non-reactive. Although strong, they can be easily shaped. These metals are also good at conducting electricity, especially silver and copper. They are often used in electronics for this reason.

Group 2 Elements Elements such as magnesium and calcium are also metals. They, too, are shiny, but they are also very reactive with oxygen. Magnesium burns so much in air that it is used in flares because of the bright light it produces. Several elements in this group create the different colors you see in fireworks.

Group 18 Elements The noble gases are special because they are not very reactive with other substances. Argon was used to replace the air inside light bulbs because it would not react with the metal inside. Helium is lighter than air, so it is used to make balloons float. It is not as light as hydrogen gas, but its nonreactivity makes it safer to use.

21. Why do substances of copper, magnesium, and helium have different properties?

(br) ©D. Hurst/Alamy

Different Structures from the Same Types of Atoms

Substances with different types of atoms have different properties. But substances with the same type of atoms can also have different properties if the atoms are arranged differently.

Molecular Structure of Oxygen and Ozone

Oxygen and ozone gases are made up of the same type of atom—oxygen—but they are completely different substances. Both occur in the atmosphere and are important for life on Earth. We need to breathe in oxygen to live. So do animals. Oxygen is also an essential ingredient to make fire. Ozone absorbs ultraviolet radiation. Its presence in the atmosphere acts as a protective layer so less of this damaging radiation reaches Earth's surface. Ozone can also be used to sterilize drinking water.

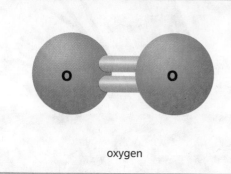

oxygen

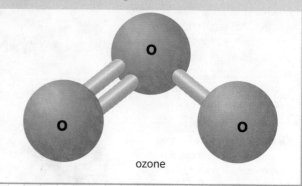

ozone

22. **Discuss** What might explain differences in properties between oxygen and ozone when both substances are made of the same type of atoms?

Diamond and Graphite

Diamond and graphite are both made of carbon atoms. However, they have different properties because their atoms are arranged in different ways. Diamonds are very hard. Cut and polished diamonds bounce light in different directions. Graphite is a dark, dull gray and easily rubs off onto paper.

diamond

graphite

23. What could explain the differences in diamond and graphite? Both substances are made of the same / different atoms. The atoms are arranged in the same / a different way in each substance. So, the atoms form the same / different substances.

Molecular Structure of Diamond and Graphite

The substance diamond is made of carbon.	The substance graphite is also made of carbon.

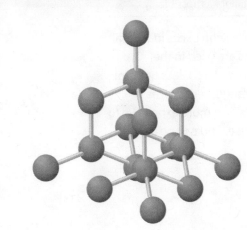	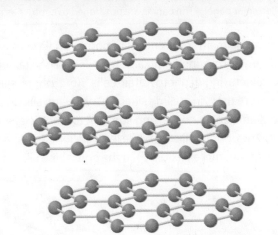

24. Diamond and graphite are both pure carbon. They are both pure substances made of carbon atoms, but the atoms are arranged in different ways. Diamonds are one of the hardest substances on Earth. Graphite is very soft and will easily break apart. What is it about the structure of graphite that might explain its properties?

A. The layered structure of graphite causes the bonds between atoms to strengthen.

B. Graphite is soft because its structure causes the individual atoms to bend.

C. The layered structure of graphite allows the layers to slide past each other.

D. Graphite breaks apart easily because its atoms cause graphite to be dark in color.

 EVIDENCE NOTEBOOK

25. How can the arrangement of atoms help explain how the white phosphorus and red phosphorus can both be pure phosphorus substances? Record your evidence.

Engineer It

Evaluate Cost vs. Performance

We use energy every day. For example, in our homes we use electrical energy to heat up a room or turn on the TV. One of the cleanest sources of energy is solar energy, which can be harnessed using photovoltaic cells. *Photo* refers to light, and *voltaic* refers to electrical energy. Photovoltaic cells directly convert sunlight to electrical energy.

Photovoltaic cells are carefully manufactured in a factory. Then they are formed into larger frames called solar panels. The panels are positioned to capture as much direct sunlight as possible.

One of the main components of photovoltaic cells is silicon. Pure silicon exists in several different forms, including amorphous and crystalline. Both forms are used in the manufacturing of photovoltaic cells. Amorphous silicon has a less ordered, less uniform structure than crystalline silicon. Crystalline silicon's ordered arrangement makes it more efficient at converting sunlight to electricial energy, but it is also more expensive to use. Amorphous silicon, while less efficient, is less expensive to use, and can be thinner, lighter, and more flexible than the crystalline silicon.

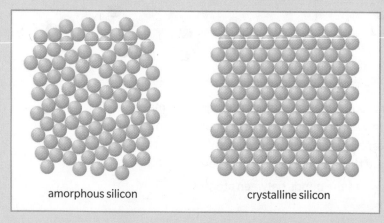

amorphous silicon   crystalline silicon

26. Assess the pros and cons of using these two materials, crystalline silicon and amorphous silicon, to manufacture photovoltaic cells. Which material would be used if the main criterion was keeping the cost of materials as low as possible? Which material would be used if the main criterion was getting the best performance from the material? Explain your reasoning.

_____

_____

_____

_____

_____

Continue Your Exploration

Name: _____ Date: _____

Check out the path below or go online to choose one of the other paths shown.

People in Science

- Hands-On Labs 🖐
- Molecules and Your Sense of Smell
- Propose Your Own Path

Go online to choose one of these other paths.

Joseph Proust, Chemist

In the 18th century and early 19th century, French chemist Joseph Proust worked and taught in France and Spain. He is best known for his work on what is called the law of definite proportions. This law states that a pure chemical compound always contains the same elements in exactly the same proportions by mass. Although many scientists assumed this to be true, it was Proust who first gathered evidence to support it.

Suppose you have a sample of sodium chloride, or table salt. You determine that the sample consists of 39% by mass of the element sodium and 61% by mass of the element chlorine, a ratio of 39% sodium to 61% chlorine. This proportion is true not only for *this* sample of sodium chloride, but *all* samples of sodium chloride. No matter where or how this pure substance is found, this proportion holds true.

The Law of Definite Proportions

As shown in the top row, 10.00 g of lead reacts with 1.55 g of sulfur to produce 11.55 g of lead sulfide. If you only add more sulfur (middle row) or only add more lead (bottom row), you will still end up with exactly 11.55 g of lead sulfide. The compound always contains the same elements in exactly the same proportion.

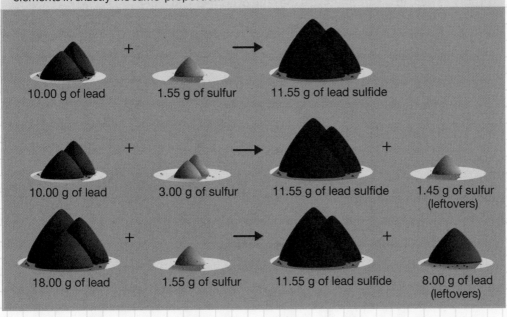

10.00 g of lead	+	1.55 g of sulfur	→	11.55 g of lead sulfide		
10.00 g of lead	+	3.00 g of sulfur	→	11.55 g of lead sulfide	+	1.45 g of sulfur (leftovers)
18.00 g of lead	+	1.55 g of sulfur	→	11.55 g of lead sulfide	+	8.00 g of lead (leftovers)

Getty Images

Continue Your Exploration

1. Why is Proust's law of definite proportions important? Why is it important to know these elemental ratios?

Copper Carbonate

Through investigation, Proust showed that copper carbonate always has 5.3 parts copper to 4 parts oxygen to 1 part carbon. In other words, the ratio of copper to oxygen to carbon is 5.3 : 4 : 1. The picture shows that in a 103 g sample of copper carbonate, there is 53 g of copper, 40 g of oxygen, and 10 g of carbon.

| 103 g of copper carbonate | 53 g of copper | 40 g of oxygen | 10 g of carbon |

2. In a sample of copper carbonate, how much copper and oxygen would there be for 5 g of carbon? Use the ratio of copper to oxygen to carbon.

3. A sample of copper carbonate was found to contain 15.9 g of copper. How many grams of copper carbonate were in the sample? Use the ratio of copper to oxygen to carbon.

4. **Collaborate** Work with a partner. Choose one of the pure samples described below. Use the periodic table to determine the mass ratio of the elements in the compound. Present your findings to the class and explain.

   • Carbon monoxide is made up of 1 atom of carbon and 1 atom of oxygen.

   • Carbon dioxide is made up of 1 carbon atom and 2 oxygen atoms.

   • Calcium carbonate is made up of 1 calcium atom, 1 carbon atom, and 3 oxygen atoms.

Can You Explain It?

Name: _____   **Date:** _____

How can both of these samples be pure phosphorus?

EVIDENCE NOTEBOOK

Refer to the notes in your Evidence Notebook to help you construct an explanation for how the two samples can both be pure phosphorus.

1. State your claim. Make sure your claim fully explains how the two samples can both be pure phosphorus.

2. Summarize the evidence you have gathered to support your claim and explain your reasoning.

Checkpoints

Answer the following questions to check your understanding of the lesson.

Use the model to answer Questions 3 and 4.

3. Which of the following can be observed from the model of water? Circle all that apply.

   A. Water is a molecule.

   B. Water is a compound.

   C. Water is made up of three types of atoms.

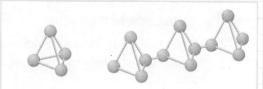

4. Another way to model water is with letters and lines is like this: H–O–H. What is one way that these two models are different?

   A. They show different types and numbers of atoms.

   B. The atoms are connected in a different order.

   C. The forces holding the atoms together are represented differently.

   D. One model clearly shows a repeating pattern.

Use the models to answer Questions 5 and 6.

5. Look carefully at the models of white phosphorus and red phosphorus. Circle the correct terms to complete each statement.

   The balls represent atoms / chemical bonds.
   The sticks represent atoms / chemical bonds.
   The two substances they represent have different
   structures / compounds. This means each
   atom / substance has different properties.

   white phosphorus   red phosphorus

6. Based on the models of these structures, white phosphorus is a(n)
   simple molecule / extended structure. Red phosphorus
   is a(n) simple molecule / extended structure. Both are
   examples of a(n) compound / element.

---

7. The structure of carbon tetrachloride, CCl_4, is similar to the structure of carbon tetrabromide, CBr_4. Both molecules have four atoms connected to a central carbon atom. Does that mean the two substances have the same properties? Choose the best explanation.

   A. Yes, because molecules with similar structures must have the same properties.

   B. Yes, because the carbon atom determines the properties of both substances.

   C. No, because the types of atoms in a molecule and its structure both influence the properties of a substance.

Interactive Review

Complete this section to review the main concepts of the lesson.

Atoms can combine to form a great variety of substances.

A. How are molecules, compounds, and pure substances related?

Models can be used to study simple molecules, complex molecules, and extended structures.

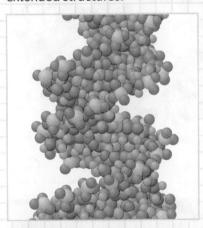

B. What do models of molecules and extended structures show?

The properties of pure substances are directly influenced by their structures.

C. What is the relationship between the structure of a substance and the properties of a substance? Explain.

Choose one of the activities to explore how this unit connects to other topics.

☐ Technology Connection

Silicon Valley Silicon Valley is the region in the San Francisco Bay Area where a large number of tech companies are based and many technological innovations are developed. Its nickname comes from the fact that the element silicon is a key component of computer chips.

Research how silicon is obtained and why its physical properties make it useful for the computer industry. Create a presentation highlighting silicon's properties and give examples of how it is used in electronic devices.

☐ Life Science Connection

Protein Power Proteins are large molecules found in all living things. Their complex structures are essential to their wide range of functions within organisms. Proteins are involved in almost every process in our bodies.

Research the structure of proteins and the biological functions in which they are involved. Create a poster that lists several of the general cellular functions of proteins. Choose a specific protein and describe what it does in the body. Include a diagram modeling the structure and function of the specific protein you chose.

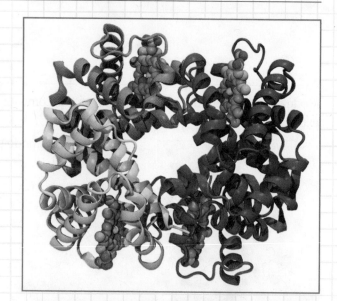

☐ Social Studies Connection

Mining on Mars NASA achieved the first flyby of our neighboring planet Mars in 1965. Additional successful missions to Mars have provided scientists with wealths of data that have vastly changed our understanding of the Red Planet.

Research the planet Mars. Is it composed of materials similar to Earth? Are any of those substances useful to humans? Does Mars have water and other resources that could allow people to live on the planet? Prepare a chart that compares the environments of Earth and Mars and describe some of the elements and compounds that have been detected on Mars.

Name: _____   Date: _____

Complete this review to check your understanding of the unit.

Use the photo of the test tube to answer Questions 1–2.

1. The liquids in the test tube float on top of each other in layers. The *least / most* dense liquids are on the bottom. The liquids lower in the tube have *less / more* mass per unit volume than the liquids in the upper part of the tube.

2. What would happen if a small, solid object with the same density as the green liquid was dropped into the test tube?

   A. It would sink to the bottom because solids have higher densities than liquids.

   B. It would sink to the same level as the green liquid and stay there because it is the same density as the green liquid.

   C. It would float on the surface because it is so small.

   D. It would sink to the same level as the white liquid and stay there because it is the same density as the green liquid.

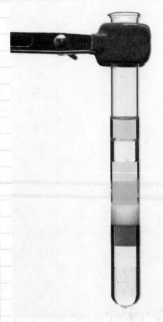

Use the diagram to answer Questions 3–5.

3. Air *is / is not* a pure substance because it is made up of *a single / more than one* type of matter.

4. Which of the following components of air is a compound?

   A. carbon dioxide

   B. oxygen

   C. nitrogen

   D. argon

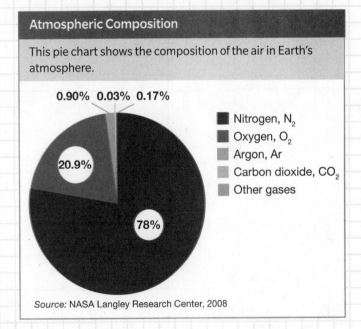

Atmospheric Composition

This pie chart shows the composition of the air in Earth's atmosphere.

0.90% 0.03% 0.17%

- Nitrogen, N_2
- Oxygen, O_2
- Argon, Ar
- Carbon dioxide, CO_2
- Other gases

20.9%

78%

Source: NASA Langley Research Center, 2008

5. A molecule of carbon dioxide is made up of a carbon atom and two oxygen atoms. Which of the following models represents carbon dioxide?

   A.

   B.

   C.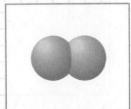

   D.

6. Complete the table by providing at least one example of how each category of matter relates to each big concept.

Matter	Scale	Structure	Everyday examples
atom	the smallest unit of an element that has the chemical identity of that element		
molecule			
compound			
crystals and extended structures			

Name: _____   Date: _____

Use the images of sodium and silver to answer Questions 7–10.

Pure sodium, Na, and pure silver, Ag, appear similar when they are in their solid forms. When sodium is added to water, an explosive reaction occurs. However, no reaction occurs when pure silver is placed in water.

sodium

sodium in water

silver

silver in water

7. Describe the physical properties of sodium and silver.

8. Describe the chemical properties of sodium and silver. Why is silver often used to make eating utensils?

9. Sodium and silver are not in the same column on the periodic table. How would you expect other elements in the same groups as sodium and silver to behave in water?

10. Compare sodium and silver before and after placing them in water. Has a new substance been produced in each case?

Use the molecular models of hydrocarbons to answer Questions 11–14.

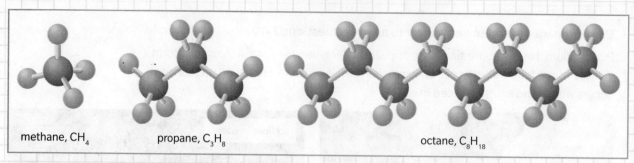

methane, CH_4 propane, C_3H_8 octane, C_8H_{18}

11. In the molecular models, the green atoms represent carbon and the blue atoms represent hydrogen. What is the ratio of carbon to hydrogen atoms in each of these molecules?

12. How many chemical bonds does each carbon atom form?

13. Hydrocarbons are often used as energy-rich fuels. When these substances are burned, the carbon bonds break and release energy. Which hydrocarbon will produce the most energy per molecule when it is burned?

14. Hydrocarbons with 4 or fewer carbon atoms are gases at room temperature, and hydrocarbons with 5–12 carbon atoms are liquids at room temperature. At what state would you expect each of these substances to exist at room temperature?

Name: _____   Date: _____

Molecular Clues!

Scientists use their knowledge of matter's structure and properties to develop new technologies and processes. Gel electrophoresis is a method used to study proteins and other large molecules. It enables scientists to separate these complex molecules based on their size and can be used in many different scientific fields, including forensics and medicine.

Research gel electrophoresis. Describe the technique and how it works, provide examples of when it is used, and design a model to demonstrate this useful technology. Then, prepare a presentation that highlights your findings.

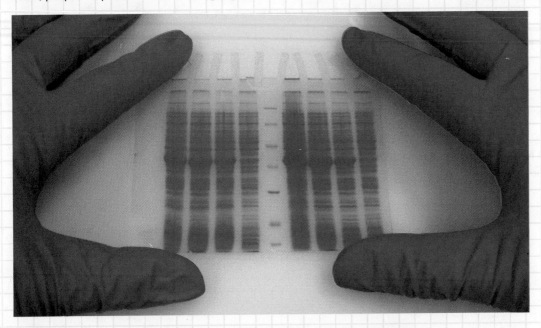

The steps below will help guide you to develop and carry out your plan.

1. **Conduct Research** Research examples of situations in which gel electrophoresis is used and the types of molecules that scientists separate using this technique.

2. **Ask a Question** How do scientists take advantage of differences between the properties of substances to make this technique work?

3. **Construct an Explanation** Based on your research, write a report that explains how gel electrophoresis works and how a scientist can interpret the results in an electrophoresis gel.

4. **Develop a Model** Create your own physical model representing how electrophoresis is used to separate substances.

5. **Communicate** Present your findings to the class, and share your model of gel electrophoresis.

✓ **Self-Check**

	I conducted research on how gel electrophoresis is used and examples of its application.
	I explained how gel electrophoresis separates molecules based on differences in their properties and how scientists can interpret the results.
	I developed a model to show how electrophoresis works.
	I communicated my results by presenting my findings to the class and sharing my model.

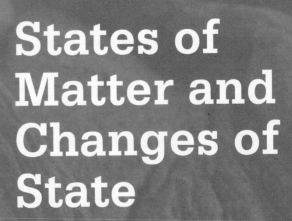

States of Matter and Changes of State

Hot gases and liquid molten material from beneath Earth's surface ooze from the Kilhauea Volcano in Hawaii. The molten material hardens to form solid rock on Earth's surface.

The matter around us commonly exists in three different forms, or states: solid, liquid, and gas. We depend on matter in each state to go about our daily lives. Liquid water covers most of Earth's surface and is essential to life. Solid materials enable us to build structures, such as homes and bridges. The air we breathe is a mixture of gases. How do we differentiate the states of matter? How does matter change from one state to another? In this unit, you will learn about the characteristics of the different states of matter and how each state of matter may change into another.

Why It Matters

Here are some questions to consider as you work through the unit. Can you answer any of the questions now? Revisit these questions at the end of the unit to apply what you discover.

Questions	Notes
Why is Earth's temperature range important to the support of life on the planet?	
Why might you need to change a recipe if you use it at a higher or lower altitude?	
How would life on Earth be different if solid water (ice) sank instead of floated?	
What role do changes of state play in cooling your body when you exercise?	
How is weather influenced by the different states of water?	
Why can it be snowing at the top of a mountain and at the same time raining at its base?	

Unit Starter: Identifying Characteristics of Matter

You are already familiar with matter in different forms. Observe these images, which show water and steel in different forms.

1. Ice cubes and steel beams are similar because they *have / do not have* a definite shape. Water poured from a bottle and molten steel are similar because they *have / do not have* a definite shape.

2. Ice is at a *lower / higher* temperature than water being poured from a bottle. Molten steel is at a *lower / higher* temperature than steel beams.

 Go online to download the Unit Project Worksheet to help you plan your project.

Unit Project

The Case of the Disappearing Arctic Sea Ice

Satellite data show that Arctic ice has been disappearing over the last 35 years. Where is it going? How does this affect climate and, ultimately, life on Earth? Channel your inner sleuth and discover why this polar ice is disappearing and where it is going.

States of Matter

Solid water provides an icy home to these penguins. They are also at home swimming in the liquid ocean water.

By the end of this lesson . . .

you will be able to describe the physical properties of solids, liquids, and gases and model particles to explain their differences.

Go online to view the digital version of the Hands-On Lab for this lesson and to download additional lab resources.

CAN YOU EXPLAIN IT?

How do these three forms of bromine differ from each other?

This container holds a single substance in three different forms at the same time. The light orange haze, the reddish-orange pool, and the bar are all forms of the element bromine.

1. Describe the differences in the three forms of bromine shown in the picture.

2. What could be the reason for these differences?

EVIDENCE NOTEBOOK As you explore the lesson, gather evidence to help explain the differences you see in the three forms of bromine.

Observing Properties of Matter

Most of the matter around you is in one of three *states*, also known as *phases* of matter—solid, liquid, or gas. Each state can be described by its physical properties of volume and shape. You can observe shape by looking carefully at a material. There are many ways to measure volume, the amount of space matter takes up. For example, you might use a graduated cylinder to measure the volume of a liquid. To classify matter as a solid, liquid, or gas, you need to observe how the volume and shape of the sample can change.

Explore
ONLINE!

Liquid aluminum is poured into molds to make solid bars.

3. Why can the liquid metal be poured into a block-shaped mold? Describe what happens to the shape and volume of the liquid metal.

4. Think of the solids and liquids that you encounter every day. In what ways are solids and liquids similar? In what ways are they different?

Hands-On Lab
Observe States of Matter

You will observe the shape of a solid and liquid in different containers. You will also investigate how the volume of a solid, liquid, and gas may change.

Procedure and Analysis

STEP 1 Draw 10 mL of air into the syringe. Record the initial volume in the table below.

STEP 2 Tighten the cap onto the end of the syringe, if one is available. Alternatively, you can press your finger against the end of the syringe to act as a cap. Push in the plunger. Record the final volume and any other observations. SAFETY NOTE: Always point the tip safely away from others when pushing in the plunger.

STEP 3 Observe the shape of the marbles in the cup. Remove the plunger and place the marbles in the syringe. Then replace the plunger so the bottom of the plunger touches the top of the marbles. Record the volume and observations.

STEP 4 Tighten the cap. Push in the plunger. Record the volume and observations.

STEP 5 Observe the shape of the water in the cup. Remove the marbles from the syringe and replace the plunger. Then draw 10 mL of water into the syringe. Record the volume and observations.

STEP 6 Tighten the cap. Push in the plunger. Record the volume and observations.

MATERIALS
- marbles, 16 mm (3), in clear plastic cup
- needleless plastic syringe with cap, 10 mL, disposable
- water in clear plastic cup

	Observations		
	Gas (air)	Solid (marbles)	Liquid (water)
Initial shape	not visible		
Shape in syringe	not visible		
Initial volume			
Final volume			
Additional observations			

STEP 7 **Do the Math** How much did the volume of the samples change when you pushed in the plunger? Based on your results for the volume of air, what might you conclude about the shape of air in the syringe? Explain.

STEP 8 Which patterns did you observe that help to classify any matter as a solid, liquid, or gas? Compare the observations that you made for the solid, liquid, and gas samples of matter. Write *can* or *cannot* to make each statement true.

Gases _____ change shape and _____ change volume.

Liquids _____ change shape and _____ change volume.

Solids _____ change shape and _____ change volume.

Solids, liquids, and gases can be classified by their abilities to change their shape and volume. A **solid** is the state of matter in which the volume and shape of a substance are fixed. A **liquid** is the state of matter that has a fixed volume, but can change shape. A **gas** is the state of matter that can change both shape and volume. Liquids and gases take the shape of their container, while solids have a definite shape. Only gases can change their volume.

 EVIDENCE NOTEBOOK

5. How do your observations of the solid, liquid, and gas samples help you describe the differences in the three forms of bromine? Record your evidence.

 Engineer It

Identify Patterns in Shape and Volume

6. Properties of matter affect how people need to handle the different states of matter, such as the propane gas that is being carried inside this tanker truck. Look at the tank of the truck that contains the gas. Why is this tank design useful for transporting a gas? Considering the volume and shape properties of each state of matter, how might the container on a truck carrying a liquid or solid be designed differently?

_____
_____
_____
_____
_____
_____

Explaining Properties of Matter

Particles of Matter

All matter is made of tiny, moving particles. For any given substance, its solid, liquid, and gas forms are made up of the same kinds of particles. So, what exactly is a particle? In gases, solids, and liquids, a particle may be a molecule or an atom. For example, water in any state is made up of the same water molecules. Some gases, such as the helium inside a balloon, are made of single atoms. Some solids, such as table salt or the minerals in rocks, are made of subunits of atoms that are connected in a specific pattern that repeats throughout the solid.

Even though a given substance is made up of the same specific kind of atoms, molecules, or subunits of atoms, those particles have different amounts of motion in each state. These differences in particle motion affect whether the attraction between particles keeps the particles close together or not. This is why certain properties of matter depend on the state of matter.

The rock and the flowing lava are both made of the same kinds of particles.

7. What states of rock can you see in the photo?

8. Discuss Think about the properties you have observed for solids, liquids, and gases. How might the arrangement and motion of the particles in each state result in these properties? Together with a partner or small group, describe or draw how you would model the particles for the same amount of a solid, liquid, and gas.

Model Particles in Solids, Liquids, and Gases

Kinetic energy is the energy of motion. A moving car has kinetic energy, and its kinetic energy increases as its speed increases.

The particles that make up matter also have kinetic energy. In all states of matter, even solids, the particles are in constant motion. However, the particles move in different ways in each state. As the motion of the particles increases, their kinetic energy also increases. Look at each model below to see how the particle spacing and motion differs in each state of matter.

9. Write gas, liquid, or solid to label the state that each model shows.

Particles are closely spaced and in contact with each other in a structured pattern. Particles vibrate in place without changing their place in the structure.

_____

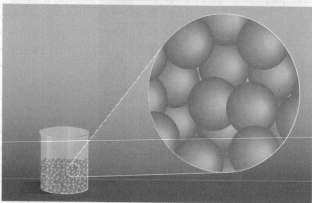

Particles are closely spaced and in contact with each other. Particles move past and around each other, so they change relative locations as they move.

_____

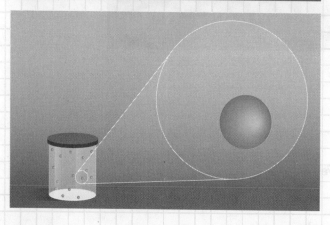

Particles are spaced far apart and only occasionally collide with each other. Particles change location relative to each other constantly because they are moving quickly.

_____

EVIDENCE NOTEBOOK

10. How could kinetic energy, particle motion, and particle attraction help explain the differences in the three forms of bromine? Record your evidence as you complete the lesson.

11. Language SmArts Use what you have observed and learned about each state of matter to describe the characteristics of a solid, liquid, and gas. Write yes or no to complete the table.

Characteristics		Solid	Liquid	Gas
Shape	fixed shape			no
	shape changes to fit container			
Volume	fixed volume	yes		
	volume changes to fit container			
Particle motion	vibrate in place		no	
	slide past each other, change relative locations			
	move freely, change relative locations			
Kinetic energy	has a low kinetic energy			
	has a medium kinetic energy	no	yes	no
	has a high kinetic energy			

12. Attractions between particles hold the particles of liquids and solids close together. Why is the attraction that particles have for each other not enough to keep gas particles close together? Does the number of particles change as a gas spreads out?

13. Use what you have learned about particle attraction and kinetic energy. Write increases or decreases to label each arrow.

kinetic energy _____

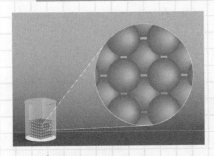  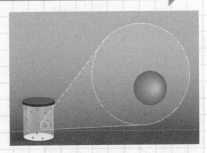

influence of particle attraction _____

Particles in Motion

The particles in matter are always moving, which means that the particles have kinetic energy. In a gas, the particles of a substance are far apart, move in all directions, and constantly change their relative locations. The attraction between particles has the least influence on gas particles because they have the most kinetic energy. In a liquid, the kinetic energy is less, so the influence of particle attraction is greater in a liquid than in a gas. This means that liquid particles can still move from place to place, but they are close together. Particles in a solid are held close together and can only vibrate back and forth in one place. This is because particles in a solid have the least kinetic energy, and so they are most influenced by particle attraction.

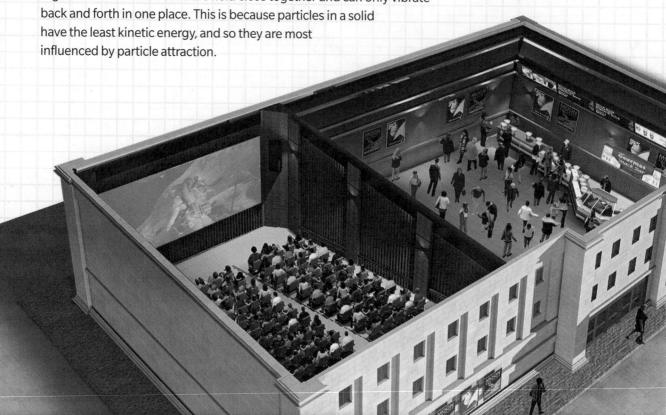

Make Analogies for Particles in Motion

14. Think about what you know about the motion and spacing of the particles in each state of matter. How can this illustration of people at the theater be used as a model of solids, liquids, and gases? Explain which group of people best represents the particles in a solid, liquid, and gas.

_____

_____

_____

_____

_____

_____

_____

15. **Act** Together as a group, act out a classroom scenario to model how the arrangement of particles differs between solids, liquids, and gases.

Continue Your Exploration

Name: _____ **Date:** _____

Check out the path below or go online to choose one of the other paths shown.

| Why Does Ice Float? | • Plasma—A Fourth State of Matter • Propose Your Own Path | *Go online to choose one of these other paths.* |

Most Liquids and Solids

Particles that make up solids have attractions to each other that hold the particles very close in fixed positions. Particles in liquids have more kinetic energy, so they are able to move around more, but they are still held very close. In most substances, the particles in a liquid state are a bit farther apart than they are in a solid state. Because liquid particles are not packed as tightly together, the solid state of a substance takes up less space than the same mass of the liquid state. As a result, a solid state is denser than a liquid state. This difference in density means that a piece of solid will generally sink to the bottom of a liquid of the same substance.

A solid cube of oil sinks to the bottom of liquid oil. The solid is denser than the liquid.

A solid cube of ice floats in liquid water. The solid is less dense than the liquid.

1. Why are most substances denser in the solid state than in the liquid state?

A. Particles in a solid are smaller.

B. Particles in a solid have more mass.

C. Particles in a solid have no kinetic energy.

D. The same number of particles in a solid are arranged into a smaller space.

Continue Your Exploration

Liquid and Solid Water

Water does not follow the predicted pattern of density that is found in most other substances. Remember, the ice cube floats in water, while the oil cube sinks in oil. If the solid ice were denser than liquid water, it would sink. But it did not sink, which means that ice is less dense than liquid water.

As with other substances, the water molecules vibrate back and forth in ice and slip past one another in liquid water. Ice is similar to many solids because water molecules are arranged in a specific pattern that repeats throughout ice. However, this pattern differs from the pattern of particles in most solids because the spacing between water particles in ice is greater than spacing between water particles in liquid water. As a result, fewer water molecules in ice are packed into the same amount of space compared to liquid water. So, ice is less dense than liquid water.

2. These two particle models show water molecules in ice and in liquid water. Write solid water or liquid water to label the models.

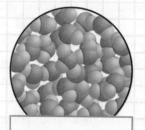 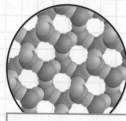

Water on Earth

The lower density of ice compared to liquid water does not only mean that ice cubes float in your water cup. It is important for life on Earth because both liquid water and ice are part of Earth's hydrosphere. The hydrosphere, which covers most of Earth's surface, is an essential part of the Earth system. It interacts with the atmosphere and biosphere in many ways. For example, large pieces of floating ice provide penguins, polar bears, and walruses with a resting place as they look for food in the ocean.

3. How would the Earth system be different if ice sank in liquid water? For example, what happens in the hydrosphere and biosphere in a lake when ice forms at the top of the lake? What might happen instead if ice were denser than liquid water?

4. **Collaborate** With a partner, discuss your ideas about what would happen to an icy lake in the winter if ice were denser than liquid water. Come to an agreement about what would happen and draw a model of the lake with ice that is denser than liquid water. Then share your ideas and model with the class.

Can You Explain It?

Name: _____   **Date:** _____

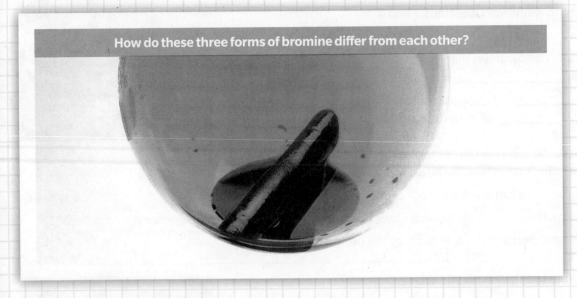

How do these three forms of bromine differ from each other?

EVIDENCE NOTEBOOK

Refer to the notes in your Evidence Notebook to help you construct an explanation for the differences seen in the three forms of bromine.

1. State your claim. Make sure your claim fully explains why the three forms of bromine are different.

2. Summarize the evidence you have gathered to support your claim and explain your reasoning.

Checkpoints

Answer the following questions to check your understanding of the lesson.

Use the photo to answer Questions 3 and 4.

3. Write shape or volume to complete each sentence.

   The photo demonstrates that liquids can change _____.

   The _____ of the spilled milk is the same as the _____ of the milk that was in the glass to start.

4. Why does the milk flow out of the glass and spread out into a thin puddle rather than staying in the glass or spreading out more across the floor?

   A. The particles can break apart but cannot move.

   B. The particles can slide past each other, but attractions hold them close together.

   C. The particles cannot move, but they can grow in size.

Use the photo to answer Questions 5–7.

5. How can the volume of gas in the balloons be greater than the volume of the cylinder used to fill them?

   A. A gas has a fixed shape.

   B. A gas expands to fill its container.

   C. The volume of the container does not depend on the gas.

6. How can the properties of the particles in a gas explain why the volume of the balloons is greater than the volume of the container?

   A. The gas particles are bigger in the balloons.

   B. The distance between the gas particles is greater in the balloons.

   C. The gas particles are locked in place in the cylinder, but can move in any direction inside the balloons.

7. If the gas cylinder is empty after all of the balloons are filled, how does the total number of particles in all the balloons compare to the total number of particles that were in the cylinder?

   A. There are more particles in the balloons than were in the cylinder.

   B. There are fewer particles in the balloons than were in the cylinder.

   C. The number of particles in the balloons is the same as the number of particles that was in the cylinder.

8. A student drew a model showing particles that are close together in a regular pattern. Which sample has the student most likely drawn a model of?

   A. a bar of gold   **C.** an air sample

   B. molten aluminum   **D.** bromine gas

Interactive Review

Complete this section to review the main concepts of the lesson.

Solids, liquids, and gases can be classified by their abilities to change their shape and volume.

A. What properties do liquids share with solids? What properties do liquids share with gases?

Differences in particle energy, motion, and arrangement explain the observed differences in the properties of solids, liquids, and gases.

B. Complete the chart to describe differences in a solid, liquid, and gas.

	Solid	Liquid	Gas
Particle arrangement			
Particle motion			
Particle energy			

(b) ©Westend61 GmbH/Alamy

Changes of State

As outdoor temperatures rise, icebergs may start to melt.

By the end of this lesson . . .

you will be able to model and explain how a change in thermal energy can influence a change of state.

CAN YOU EXPLAIN IT?

What could cause a piece of metal to melt in a person's hand?

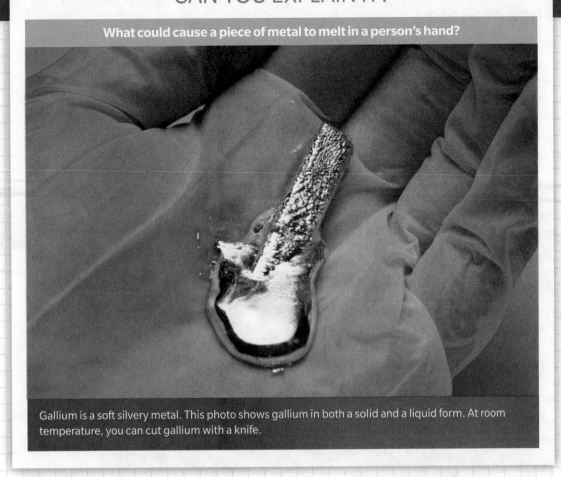

Gallium is a soft silvery metal. This photo shows gallium in both a solid and a liquid form. At room temperature, you can cut gallium with a knife.

1. Think about some times you have seen a substance melting. What explanation can you suggest for how the gallium could melt in someone's hand?

EVIDENCE NOTEBOOK As you explore the lesson, gather evidence to help explain how a piece of metal could melt in someone's hand.

Analyzing How Energy Influences a Change of State

Changes of State

All matter can exist in three common states, or phases—solid, liquid, and gas—and can change from one state to another. The process by which matter changes from one state to another is called a **change of state**. A change of state is a physical change, so the identity of a substance is the same in whatever state it is in. For example, water is still water whether in an ice cube or after the ice melts into liquid water.

During a change of state, matter is neither created nor destroyed. The same number of particles make up a substance before and after a change of state.

Explore ONLINE!

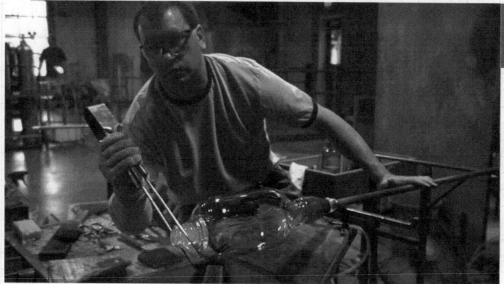

A professional glassworker creates a vase by changing the shape of the glass.

2. **Discuss** Together with a partner, determine the change of state that is shown in the photo. What observations led to your conclusion?

3. Think about what takes place when glass changes from the liquid phase to the solid phase. Circle the correct words to make each sentence true.

Liquid glass and solid glass have the same / different chemical identity.

Liquid glass and solid glass have the same / different physical properties.

Hands-On Lab
Investigate a Change of State

You will predict ways in which you can make a change of state happen more quickly as an ice cube melts. You will plan and carry out an investigation to test your predictions.

Procedure

STEP 1 Work with a partner or small group to list ways that you might make an ice cube melt faster than it would melt if you left it sitting in a cup on your desk. You may only use items in your classroom.

STEP 2 For your investigation, choose three of the methods your group discussed. Write each method in the table.

STEP 3 Gather the ice cubes. Place one ice cube in a cup on your desk. Use the methods you chose in Step 1 to melt the other three ice cubes.

STEP 4 Observe the ice cubes until one of them melts completely.

STEP 5 Record your observations in the table.

What did you do?	What were the results?
ice cube in a cup, on desk	

Analysis

STEP 6 Circle the best word to complete each sentence.

In this activity, energy was *added / removed* to make the ice cube melt faster.

The ice cube that received the *most / least* energy melted fastest.

STEP 7 Describe two actions that are different from what you did in this activity that might make the ice melt more quickly. Explain your reasoning.

EVIDENCE NOTEBOOK

4. How does energy relate to the question of how a piece of metal might melt in someone's hand? Record your evidence.

Identify a Change of State

5. This glass of ice water shows two changes of state happening:

   • The solid ice in the glass is melting to form liquid water.

   • Water vapor in the air is changing to liquid water on the surface of the glass.

Write *gaining* or *losing* to complete each sentence.

The ice is melting in the glass because it is

_____ energy as it changes from solid to liquid.

Water drops form on the surface of the glass because water vapor is _____ energy as it changes from gas to liquid.

Modeling Addition of Thermal Energy to a Substance

Energy Gain and Change of State

Each particle in a substance is moving in some way, so each particle has *kinetic energy*. **Thermal energy** is the total kinetic energy of all the particles in a substance. Adding thermal energy to a substance increases its kinetic energy. This increase in kinetic energy means the particles move faster. *Temperature* is a measure of the average kinetic energy of the particles.

6. Explain what is happening to the movement and kinetic energy of the water particles shown in the photo.

A flame adds energy to the water in this flask. As a result, the water temperature increases.

Change of State: Solid to Liquid

Adding enough thermal energy to a substance can cause a change of state to occur. The change of state from a solid to a liquid is called *melting*. When energy is added to an ice cube, the ice particles speed up as energy is absorbed. When the particles move fast enough, the solid ice melts and becomes liquid water. The temperature at which melting begins is called the *melting point*. Every substance has a specific melting point. This melting point will always be the same for that substance under the same conditions no matter the amount of the substance. The temperature at which ice melts and becomes liquid water is 0 °C at sea level.

Change of State: Liquid to Gas

If enough energy is added to a liquid, the liquid will turn into a gas. A change of state from a liquid to a gas is called *evaporation*. Water in a gas state is called *water vapor*. Adding thermal energy to liquid water particles causes them to speed up. When they speed up enough, the particles change to the gas state, forming bubbles. The liquid water turns to water vapor. This process is called *boiling*. Boiling and evaporation both involve the same change of state: liquid to gas. The difference is the location of the change. Evaporation takes place at the surface of the liquid and can occur over a wide range of temperatures. Boiling occurs throughout the entire liquid and takes place at a specific temperature. All substances have their own *boiling point*, the temperature at which the substance begins to boil. The boiling point of water is 100 °C at sea level.

7. Write melting, evaporation, or boiling to label each photo.

(bl) ©iStockPhoto.com; (bc) ©ntstudio/Shutterstock; (br) ©Houghton Mifflin Harcourt

Change of State from Solid to Liquid

The particles of a solid vibrate in place, held together by forces of attraction. Particles in a liquid remain close, but they have more kinetic energy, which means they have more freedom of movement.

Change of State from Liquid to Gas

The particles in a gas have enough energy to overcome attractive forces, so they move about freely.

8. Describe the relationship between thermal energy and change of state. Write solid, liquid, or gas to complete each sentence.

Explore ONLINE!

If enough thermal energy is added to a liquid, it will change to a

_____.

If enough thermal energy is added to a _____, it will change to a liquid.

Particle Motion Increases

The particles of a solid are held together by strong forces of attraction. As a result, a solid has a definite shape. As thermal energy is added to a solid, the kinetic energy of its particles increases. The particles vibrate faster until they can move more freely, slide around each other, and become a liquid. This freedom of movement allows a liquid to flow and take the shape of its container.

When thermal energy is added to the liquid, its particle movement increases until the particles have enough energy to overcome the attractive forces. They completely break away from each other and become a gas. The movement of the gas particles not only allows the gas to take the shape of its container, but the gas particles will also move about and fill the entire space within its container.

Do the Math
Analyze Temperature During a Change of State

Think about warming a piece of ice. The ice gains energy and its temperature rises as the motion of the particles increases. The rise in temperature causes the ice to melt and eventually boil. This is true for ice just as it is true for any substance. What would the graph of temperature change over time look like?

You might have thought that the temperature would steadily increase as energy is added to a substance at a constant rate. However, that is not the case. The graph actually shows two time periods where the temperature does not change even though energy is being added. The first corresponds to the temperature at which the solid is changing to a liquid, or melting. The second shows the temperature at which the substance is changing to a gas, or boiling. The horizontal lines indicate that, during that time, energy transferred to the particles goes into changing the state of the substance, not into raising its temperature.

9. Which statements correctly describe what is happening during the two flat-line periods in the graph? Circle all that apply.

   A. Between points A and B, the solid substance is changing to a liquid.

   B. Between points A and B, the substance is losing energy.

   C. Between points C and D, the liquid substance is changing to a gas.

   D. Between points C and D, the substance is gaining energy.

10. You are warming a pot of ice. Explain what happens to the temperature when the water reaches its melting point and boiling point.

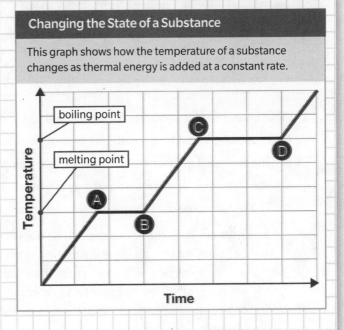

Changing the State of a Substance

This graph shows how the temperature of a substance changes as thermal energy is added at a constant rate.

EVIDENCE NOTEBOOK

11. How might melting point and a change in the kinetic energy of particles help to explain why a piece of metal could melt in someone's hand? Record your evidence.

Classify and Explain a Change of State

Snow is made up of frozen water molecules in the form of ice. As the temperature warms up, the snow begins to melt and run off as liquid water.

12. What changes might occur as sunlight shines on snow? Circle all that apply.

   A. Liquid water that forms as the snow melts will flow downhill.

   B. The snow will get warmer and change into a large chunk of ice.

   C. The snow quickly warms up and may begin to boil.

   D. The temperature of the snow will slowly increase.

 13. **Engineer It** Some towns depend on water from snow that falls high up in the mountains, melts, and flows down the mountain. Some years, spring comes early and the snow begins to melt earlier than usual. What are some problems of early water run off down the mountain that engineers might be asked to solve? What criteria and constraints might need to be considered for concerns such as materials, space, and cost?

_____

_____

_____

_____

_____

_____

_____

_____

_____

Modeling Removal of Thermal Energy from a Substance

Energy Loss and Change of State

You now know that when enough energy is added to a substance, it can change state. But what happens when a substance loses energy? Think about what happens when you put water in a freezer. The temperature of the liquid water is warmer than the temperature inside the freezer. As a result, energy from the water is lost to the freezer. When this happens, the water particles slow down. When enough energy is lost, the attractive forces between the particles hold the particles in a regular pattern and the particles can only vibrate in place. The liquid water changes to solid ice.

Explore ONLINE!

In the winter, ice forms on this lake. The ice starts to form on the water closest to shore.

Over the course of the winter, the lake continues to freeze. Eventually, most of the lake is covered in ice.

14. The photos show the process of a lake freezing in the winter. Why does the lake water change to ice in the winter? Include the gain or loss of energy in your explanation.

Change of State: Gas to Liquid

A gas changes state and becomes a liquid when the gas particles lose thermal energy. The process of a gas changing state to a liquid is called *condensation*. A common example of condensation is the picture you saw earlier of the liquid water droplets on the outside of the glass of ice water. Water vapor from the air condenses and becomes liquid water on the cold surface of the glass of ice water.

Change of State: Liquid to Solid

The process in which a liquid changes to a solid is called *freezing*. Many people might think that freezing means liquid water turning into ice. However, freezing is the term used to describe any change from a liquid state to a solid state.

Think again about water being placed in a freezer. The liquid water freezes to become solid ice. The temperature at which water freezes is its *freezing point*. The freezing point of a substance is the same as its melting point. In other words, a substance with a melting point of 20 °C will not only begin to freeze at 20 °C, but the solid substance will also begin to melt at 20 °C.

15. Write freezing or condensation to label each photo.

a dripping faucet on a cold day

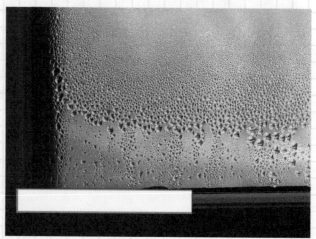

a window on a cold day

your breath in cold air

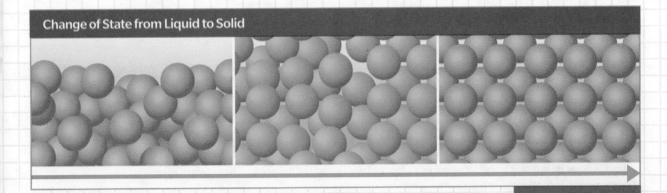

Change of State from Liquid to Solid

▷ *Explore ONLINE!*

16. The process being modeled is condensation / freezing.

    As the particles slow down / speed up, particle attraction forces hold them in a regular pattern.

    This causes the particles to lock into the fixed arrangement of a liquid / solid.

    The change in particle motion happens because of a(n) increase / decrease in kinetic energy.

    This change in average kinetic energy also results in a(n) increase / decrease in temperature.

Particle Motion Decreases

As the temperature of a substance becomes colder, its properties change. The reason is the change in particle motion. The particles in a gas have a high amount of energy and move very fast. As thermal energy decreases, particle motion slows, allowing the attractive forces between particles to pull them closer together. Gas particles will become liquid. If temperatures continue to decrease, the attraction between particles eventually overcomes the energy of their motion. Liquid particles are then locked into the fixed arrangement of a solid.

 Language SmArts

17. **Draw** In the space below or on a piece of paper, finish the drawing to show the process of gas particles becoming a liquid. Add a caption to describe what happens to the particle motion and energy during this change of state.

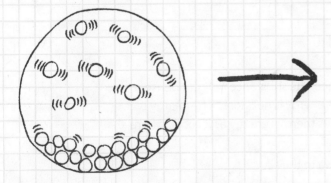

Gas particles are far apart and moving quickly above the surface of the liquid because gas particles have enough energy to overcome particle attraction.

Analyze Changes of State

Lava is liquid rock that comes out of the opening of a volcano in Earth's surface. It sometimes comes out in streams called lava flows that travel slowly downhill. The temperature of lava when it first erupts can vary between 700 °C–1,200 °C. As the lava flows, it slowly cools.

Explore ONLINE!

Lava Flowing Into the Ocean

As lava flows downhill, it sometimes reaches a body of water, such as the ocean. These two photos show what happens as the lava spills into the water.

time

18. What changes of state do you see happening in the photos?

_____

_____

_____

_____

_____

19. What evidence do you see in the photos to support your answer?

_____

_____

_____

_____

_____

20. When thermal energy is removed from a substance, the substance may condense or freeze. But when something loses energy, that energy is not "lost." The energy is transferred to something else. When the lava loses thermal energy as it cools, where is the energy going? Circle all that apply.

  A. The thermal energy is transferred from the lava to the air.

  B. The thermal energy is transferred from the lava to the ground.

  C. The thermal energy is transferred from the lava to the water.

  D. The thermal energy is held within the solid rock that forms.

Evaluating How Pressure Can Affect Changes of State

Pressure

As gas particles move freely, they collide with surfaces around them. The gas particles have kinetic energy, so their collisions with surfaces produce a force. The force created by the collisions of these particles with other materials is called **pressure**.

In the morning, this bike rider gets ready to go for a long bike ride. As part of getting ready, she is checking the tire pressure.

The bike rider finishes her ride in the afternoon. She checks the tire pressure again.

21. Use the pictures. Circle the correct word to complete each sentence.

The tire pressure changed between morning and afternoon. In the afternoon, the tire pressure was less / greater than the tire pressure in the morning. This change in pressure is caused by a warmer / cooler temperature of the air in the tires compared to morning. As the temperature increases, the kinetic energy of the gas particles increases / decreases.

Elevation and Air Pressure

You might not think about the pressure that air puts on your body, but it is always present. Gas particles in the atmosphere exert pressure on everything, including you.

The art shows that as you move toward a higher elevation, there are not as many air particles to collide with a surface. As a result, the higher the elevation, the lower the air pressure. Air at lower elevations contains a greater number of air particles, resulting in a greater number of particle collisions with the ground and other surfaces. Therefore, lower elevations have greater air pressure.

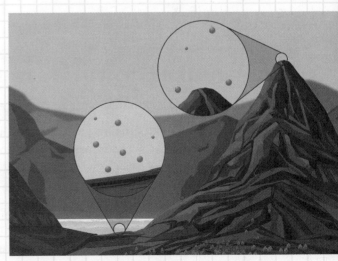

The air at lower elevations contains more particles in a given amount of space than air at higher elevations.

Pressure and Changes of State

Even if the kinetic energy of particles does not change, a change of state can occur when there is a change in pressure. The relationship between a change in pressure and a change of state is especially noticeable for the changes that occur between the liquid and gas states.

If you increase the pressure on a substance, its particles are brought closer to each other. When this happens to a gas, attractive forces may be strong enough to hold the particles close together and the gas can condense into a liquid.

When the pressure on a substance is decreased, particles can move farther apart from each other. Fewer collisions occur, putting less force on the particles. With less force acting on the particles, it takes less energy for a liquid to change into a gas. With less air pressure on the surface of a liquid, particles can move from the liquid state to the gas state with less energy than that change would require at a higher pressure.

Boiling Point of Water at Different Elevations			
Location	Elevation (feet above sea level)	Pressure (in atmospheres)	Boiling point of water (°C)
San Francisco, CA	sea level	1.0	100.0
Denver, CO	5,280	0.82	95.0
Quito, Ecuador	9,350	0.71	90.0
Mount Everest	29,029	0.31	76.5

22. **Discuss** Water boils at 100 °C in San Francisco, which is at sea level. But as you can see in the table, the boiling point of water varies at other locations.

Consider this scenario: You are at sea level. You have some liquid water at 80 °C. What would happen to the water if it was suddenly transported to an elevation of 29,029 feet above sea level? Why would this happen? Work with a group to explain. Include the relationship of pressure, energy, and change of state in your explanation.

Determine the Effect of Pressure on a Change of State

23. In Denver, it takes about 4 minutes to make a soft-boiled egg. At sea level, it takes about 3 minutes and 11 seconds to make a soft-boiled egg. Why does it take more time to soft-boil an egg in Denver than at sea level? Write higher or lower to complete the explanation.

Denver is at a _____ elevation than sea level, so water boils at a _____ temperature. In Denver, food must be cooked longer to make up for cooking with a _____ temperature.

Continue Your Exploration

Name: _____   Date: _____

Check out the path below or go online to choose one of the other paths shown.

Careers in Science

- **Hands-On Labs**
- **Freezing Point Depression**
- **Propose Your Own Path**

Go online to choose one of these other paths.

Forensics

A scientist who analyzes evidence and presents data in a court of law is called a forensic scientist. Forensic scientists apply scientific knowledge and procedures to criminal investigations. They may analyze clues from crime scenes or accident scenes. Forensic scientists are able to help solve crimes using scientific analysis.

Evidence is collected at a crime scene. Just looking at an item may not tell an investigator much. However, an expert in a crime lab can learn more from a detailed analysis of the evidence.

---

1. Which of the following processes would a forensic scientist use? Circle all that apply.

   A. analyzing fragments to determine what they are made of

   B. analyzing paint flecks to determine the color and chemical makeup

   C. identifying the identity of a person based on a shoe print

   D. identifying a substance that was found on a fiber

   E. determining whether liquids found are the same or different

Continue Your Exploration

Analyzing the Evidence

Gas chromatography (GC) is a method used to identify certain chemicals. A tiny bit of a sample is dissolved in a liquid called the solvent. The liquid is then injected into a chamber where the sample is heated until it becomes a gas. The gas travels through a long, thin tube. The different chemicals that make up the sample travel at different rates because of their different properties. A sensor sees when a chemical passes and records the time. The scientist can identify each chemical by the amount of time it takes to pass through the gas chromatograph.

Scientists can use GC to make sure that the chemical composition of a product is correct, to identify pollutants, or to identify unknown substances in a crime scene sample.

2. Circle the statement that best describes the process that happens in the heated sample chamber of a gas chromatograph.

   A. The sample melts and becomes a gas.

   B. The sample boils and becomes a gas.

   C. The sample condenses and becomes a gas.

When using gas chromatography to identify an unknown sample, a scientist first prepares a standard that contains known chemicals. The standard is analyzed to see how long it takes those chemicals to go through the gas chromatograph. By comparing the results for the unknown sample with a standard of known chemicals, the identity of the unknown sample can be determined.

A forensic scientist has been asked to examine a fiber from the scene of a fire. Gas chromatography was used to identify oil found on the fiber. The analysis of the sample is shown in the chromatogram. From the results, the scientist determined that the sample was linseed oil. Linseed oil is commonly used as paint thinner and is very flammable.

3. How might knowing that the material on the fiber was paint thinner help an investigator solve a crime?

Chromatogram of the Evidence Sample

The different peaks are used to identify the solvent, substances in the sample, and their amounts.

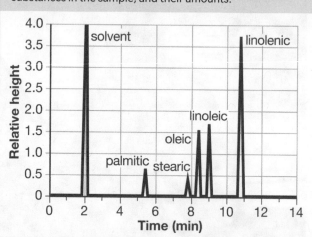

4. **Collaborate** Work with a partner to put together a brief presentation for the class about how forensic scientists use chemical analysis to help solve crimes. Use some kind of technology in your presentation to support your idea, such as presentation software, a video link, or digital photos.

Can You Explain It?

Name: _____   Date: _____

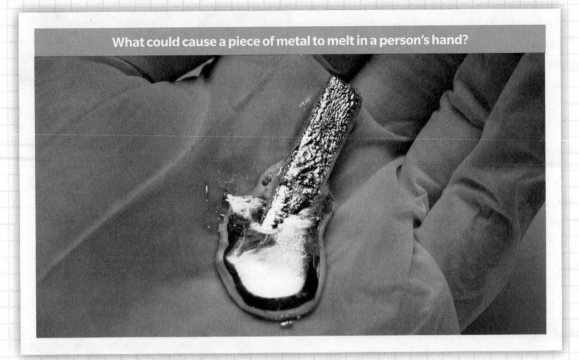

What could cause a piece of metal to melt in a person's hand?

EVIDENCE NOTEBOOK

Refer to the notes in your Evidence Notebook to help you construct an explanation for what could cause a piece of metal to melt in someone's hand.

1. State your claim. Make sure your claim fully explains how the gallium could melt.

2. Summarize the evidence you have gathered to support your claim and explain your reasoning.

Checkpoints

Answer the following questions to check your understanding of the lesson.

Use the photo to answer Questions 3 and 4.

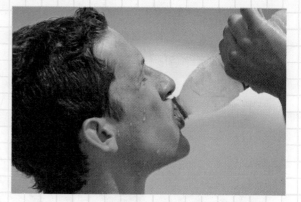

3. Sweating is one way the body cools itself. Circle the statement that best explains this cooling process.

   A. Water condenses on the skin, adding thermal energy to the body.

   B. Moisture from the body evaporates from the skin, removing thermal energy from the body.

4. Which situations model a process similar to sweating? Circle all that apply.

   A. water droplets forming on the outside of a glass of ice water

   B. a wet bandana around the neck of hiker

   C. wet clothes hanging on a clothes line

   D. a hot, moist towel placed on sore muscles to soothe them

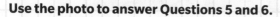

Use the photo to answer Questions 5 and 6.

5. Which weather conditions would most likely create the fog as shown in the photo?

   A. rapidly cooling air that is low in water vapor

   B. rapidly cooling air that is high in water vapor

   C. rapidly warming air that is low in water vapor

   D. rapidly warming air that is high in water vapor

6. Clouds and fog form under similar conditions. How might air pressure at higher altitudes affect the formation of clouds? Circle your answer.

   A. As air rises, the reduced pressure allows the air to expand and cool until water vapor evaporates into water droplets that form the clouds.

   B. As air rises, the reduced pressure allows the air to expand and cool until water vapor freezes into water droplets that form the clouds.

   C. As air rises, the reduced pressure allows the air to expand and cool until water vapor condenses into water droplets that form the clouds.

7. As snow slowly melts in the sunshine, what is happening to the particles of water that make up the snow? Circle all that apply.

   A. Particles are gaining energy.

   B. Particles are changing from liquid to solid.

   C. Particle motion is increasing.

Interactive Review

Complete this section to review the main concepts of the lesson.

A change of state is the change of a substance from one physical state to another, such as from a liquid to a solid.

A. Explain whether the identity of a substance changes during a change of state. Give an example.

A change of state can occur when thermal energy is added to a substance.

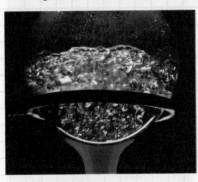

B. Describe the change in motion and kinetic energy of the particles as thermal energy is added to a liquid. Which change of state might happen?

A change of state can occur when thermal energy is removed from a substance.

C. Describe the change in motion and kinetic energy of the particles as thermal energy is removed from a liquid. Which change of state might happen?

Changes in pressure can affect changes of state.

D. Explain why liquid particles at a high pressure would need more energy to change to a gas than liquid particles at a low pressure.

Choose one of the activities to explore how this unit connects to other topics.

☐ Health Connection

Cryotherapy Modern medicine enables doctors to use some surprising tools to help their patients. One of these tools is actually quite simple. Doctors use liquid nitrogen, a substance with a very low boiling point, to treat skin conditions.

Research how liquid nitrogen is prepared and stored; be sure to find information about nitrogen's boiling point and condensation point. Describe how doctors and medical experts use liquid nitrogen to treat their patients.

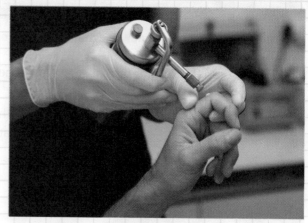

Liquid nitrogen is used to treat a skin growth.

☐ Art Connection

Working with Wax Not all "paintings" are made with paints. Some artists practice hot wax painting, also known as encaustic painting. This technique gives paintings unique characteristics quite different from traditional oil or latex paintings. It was often used for Coptic Egyptian mummy portraits.

Research encaustic painting. Describe the materials used and how artists utilize a change of state to create their artwork. Prepare a visual display and verbal presentation that describes the technique of encaustic painting. Provide several example images to share in your presentation.

An encaustic painting on the mummy of Marco Antinous.

☐ Earth Science Connection

Volcanic Islands New islands are formed by volcanic activity on Earth. High temperatures and pressure beneath Earth's surface produce chambers of molten, or liquid, rock. This molten rock can be released through volcanoes onto the Earth's surface to form new land.

Research how volcanic islands are formed. Be sure to describe the role different states of matter play in volcanic eruptions and island formation. Present your research in a multimedia presentation that includes images and descriptions of different volcanic islands.

Name: _____   Date: _____

Complete this review to check your understanding of the unit.

Use the graph to answer Questions 1–3.

1. Dew forms when the air temperature is low enough for water in the air to condense on outdoor surfaces. At what time would you expect to see dew according to the graph?

   A. 12:00 a.m.

   B. 3:00 a.m.

   C. 6:00 a.m.

   D. 12:00 p.m.

Air Temperature and Dew Point over Time

— Air temperature

— Dew point temperature

Temperature (°C) vs Time (h)

2. What would you expect to happen if the temperature dropped to below freezing after 6:00 a.m.?

   A. Dew would not form.

   B. Dew would form, but it would evaporate.

   C. Dew would form and then it would freeze, creating frost.

   D. Dew would form and then it would soak into the ground.

3. Which of the following best describes what is happening to water particles in the air during dew formation?

   A. An increase in thermal energy results in an increase in kinetic energy.

   B. A decrease in thermal energy results in a decrease in kinetic energy.

   C. An increase in thermal energy results in a decrease in kinetic energy.

   D. A decrease in thermal energy results in an increase in kinetic energy.

These are images of wet paper towels placed on a bag of room temperature water and a bag of hot water. Use the images to answer Questions 4–5.

4. The water molecules that are being heated by the hot water are moving 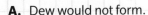 faster / slower than the water molecules on the room temperature water bag.

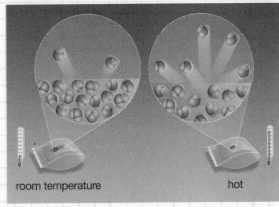

room temperature   hot

5. From which paper towel do you expect the water to evaporate first?

   A. the room temperature paper towel, because the molecules are moving slower

   B. the heated paper towel, because the molecules are moving faster

   C. The water will evaporate from both paper towels at the same time because heat does not affect the water molecules.

   D. The water will not evaporate from either paper towel.

6. Complete the table by providing a description of how the changes of state relate to each big picture concept.

Change of state	Macroscopic patterns related to the behavior of particles	Cause and effect	Energy
melting	Particles are beginning to move faster, which causes a solid to turn to a liquid.		
freezing			
boiling			
condensing			

Name: _____   **Date:** _____

Use the images of the mirrors to answer Questions 7–10.

a bathroom mirror before a hot shower

a bathroom mirror during a hot shower

7. Describe differences between the physical states of substances in the images.

8. Where did the moisture that covers the mirror in the second image come from?

9. In terms of thermal and kinetic energy, describe how water vapor forms during the hot shower.

10. In terms of thermal and kinetic energy, describe how water droplets form on the bathroom mirror.

Use the images to answer Questions 11–14.

11. The left image shows a sealed balloon that contains a chunk of dry ice (solid carbon dioxide, CO_2). The right image shows the same balloon after a short period of time. Compare the size of the balloon and amount of dry ice in each image.

12. Carbon dioxide does not exist as a liquid at normal room temperatures and pressures. It changes directly from solid to gas in a process called *sublimation*. What caused the balloon to inflate?

13. Compare the kinetic energy of carbon dioxide particles in first image to the kinetic energy of carbon dioxide particles in the second image.

14. What is the cause of this difference in kinetic energy?

Name: _____   **Date:** _____

Packed to Perfection!

Food shipment is a booming industry. The food must arrive fresh or still frozen, and the packaging must be dry and intact. Dry ice (solid carbon dioxide) and regular ice (solid water) are both used for shipping food.

You work for a small shipping company and make decisions about how to ship fresh and frozen foods to local grocery stores. Your company covers a radius of about 50 miles; it can get pretty hot during the summer months, so choosing the proper packing material is very important. Your boss has asked you to prepare a report with recommendations for shipping a variety of fresh and frozen foods:

- frozen burritos—individually packaged in plastic and shipped in cardboard boxes containing 24 burritos
- salad mix—mixed greens packaged in clear plastic containers
- fresh milk packaged in pint-sized cardboard cartons
- ice cream packaged in cardboard quart containers

Your task is to determine which shipping material—dry ice or regular ice—is best for each of the foods. Be sure to consider the cost of the packing materials and how the added weight of these materials affects shipping costs.

dry ice

regular ice

The steps below will help guide your research and develop your recommendation.

Engineer It

1. **Define the Problem** Write a statement defining the problem you are being asked to solve. Identify criteria and constraints associated with the problem.

Engineer It

2. **Conduct Research** Research the differences between dry ice and regular ice (frozen water). Research what happens when thermal energy is added (as on a hot day) to dry ice and regular ice. Compare freezing and melting points, as well as the weight and cost of equal volumes of dry ice and regular ice.

3. **Brainstorm a Solution** Discuss which material is best suited for transporting different foods. Weigh the pros and cons of each packing material. Be sure to include the cost and weight of each and how this affects the total shipping costs.

4. **Design a Model** Design a simple model or demonstration that compares the two packing materials to confirm your ideas as to which packing material is better suited for each type of food requiring refrigeration.

5. **Recommend a Solution** Based on your research and the outcome of your model or demonstration, identify which packing material you would recommend for shipping each type of food.

6. **Communicate Your Proposal** Prepare a report for your boss that highlights the reasons for the recommended packaging materials.

✓ **Self-Check**

	I defined the problem, its criteria, and its constraints.
	I researched dry ice and regular ice and learned how they change state, at what temperature this change occurs, and the weight and cost of each.
	I developed a model or demonstration to show what happens when thermal energy is added to dry ice and regular ice.
	I recommended a solution.
	I made a report to communicate my findings.

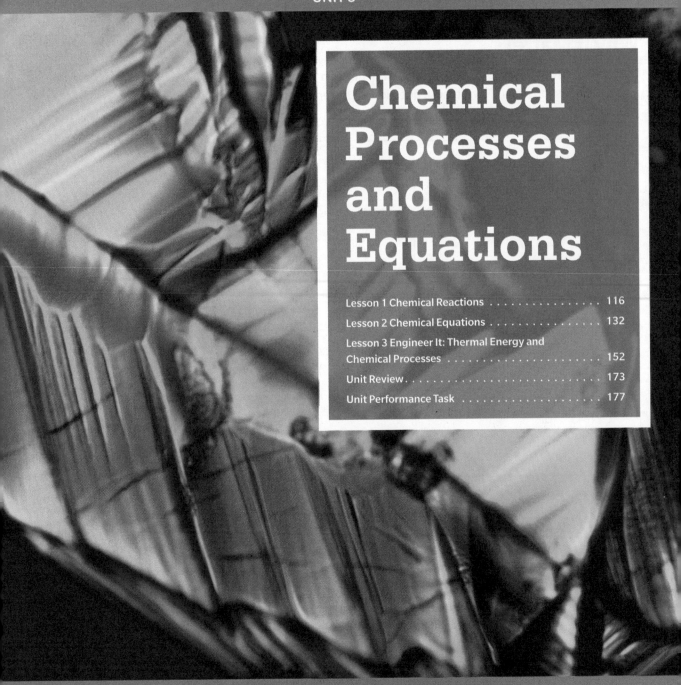

Chemical Processes and Equations

This is a crystal of progesterone, an important hormone in the human body. It can be synthetically produced from plant materials using a series of chemical reactions known as the Marker Degradation.

Chemical changes occur all around you, though you may not always notice them. You do not need to be in a laboratory to observe all kinds of reactions. A delicious cooked meal and the power supplied by the batteries in your electronic devices are both results of chemical reactions. In this unit, you will investigate how substances react to form different products and the energy involved in these changes.

Why It Matters

Here are some questions to consider as you work through the unit. Can you answer any of the questions now? Revisit these questions at the end of the unit to apply what you discover.

Questions	Notes
What are some examples of chemical reactions that occur in your everyday life?	
What are some signs that a chemical reaction is happening?	
Why do some chemical reactions happen more quickly than others?	
What does it mean for a chemical equation to be "balanced"?	
How are chemical properties different from physical properties?	

Unit Starter: Identifying Chemical Reactions

You may observe changes to the properties of materials around you in all kinds of settings. Analyze the camping scene and determine which changes result from chemical reactions.

In the fall, leaves of deciduous trees change colors before falling off the branches.

Wood is being chopped for the campfire.

The campfire is burning red-hot.

Water over the campfire is at a rolling boil.

1. Which two of these changes are chemical reactions?

   A. changing leaves

   B. chopping wood

   C. burning firewood

   D. boiling water

 Go online to download the Unit Project Worksheet to help you plan your project.

Unit Project

Design a Chemical Cold Pack

What would you do if you sprained your ankle on a hike and needed to ice the injury right away? Some chemical systems absorb energy and become cold. These can be used in portable cold packs that become cold after the components are mixed. Design two prototype cold packs, build and test them. Then analyze your results to design, build, and test an improved prototype.

Chemical Reactions

Fireflies, also called lightning bugs, are small insects that
generate their own light using chemical reactions.

By the end of this lesson . . .

you will be able to explain ways to analyze data
about substances before and after they interact to
determine whether their identities have changed.

Go online to view the digital version of
the Hands-On Lab for this lesson and to
download additional lab resources.

CAN YOU EXPLAIN IT?

What happens when sulfuric acid is added to powdered sugar?

These photos show what happens when concentrated sulfuric acid is mixed with powdered sugar.

Explore
ONLINE!

1. What do you observe when sulfuric acid is added to the powdered sugar?

2. Is the black substance that grows out of the beaker the same as the white sugar? Explain your answer.

 EVIDENCE NOTEBOOK As you explore the lesson, gather evidence to help explain what is happening when the sulfuric acid is added to the sugar.

Using Properties to Identify Substances

Properties of Matter

If someone offers you a choice of two fruits—a banana or an orange—you can make your choice based on which kind of fruit you like better. But how do you know which fruit is which? You know that a banana is long and yellow, and an orange is round and orange. You may know how each tastes. In a similar way, you can identify most substances by identifying their properties.

3. **Discuss** Iron pyrite is commonly called "fool's gold" because it looks like real gold, but it is not valuable. Both fool's gold and real gold may be found in the same area, but they have different properties. Why would it be important for a miner to know about the properties of real gold and fool's gold?

Which substance is real gold?

These two substances look similar. The one on the left is gold, but the other is a mineral called iron pyrite. One property that miners use to identify gold is density. Gold has a much higher density than iron pyrite.

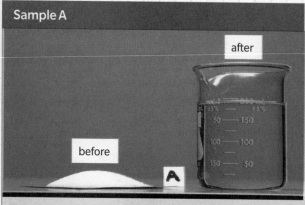

Sample A

after

before

A

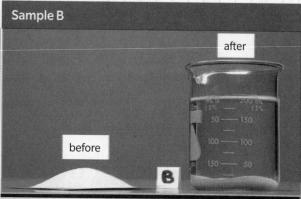

Sample B

after

before

B

Two unknown samples, Sample A and Sample B, are shown before and after they are stirred into a beaker of water.

4. Use the photos to answer the question. Are Sample A and Sample B the same substance? Explain.

Physical Properties

All substances have properties that can be used to identify the substance. The combination of properties that any substance has is unique. The more properties of a substance we can determine, the more likely we are to correctly identify that substance.

The physical properties of a substance are ones that can be observed or measured without changing the substance's identity. Physical properties include density, melting point, boiling point, color, texture, odor, solubility, malleability, and conductivity. Many more physical properties can be determined.

Every substance has a set of physical properties that are used to describe the substance. Scientists use physical properties to describe and to help identify substances. The two unknown samples in the previous photos are different substances because one substance dissolved in water and the other substance did not dissolve in water.

Chemical Properties

Another type of property, a chemical property, can be determined by observing whether or not a substance can change into another substance under a given set of conditions.

5. Use the photos to answer the question. Two nails are shown before and after being left outside in the rain. Are the two nails made of the same substance? Explain.

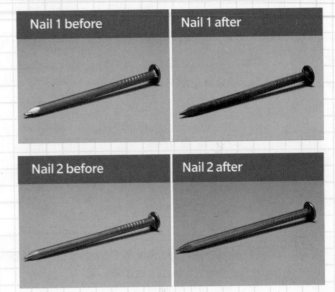

All substances also have chemical properties. Chemical properties define the ways a substance can undergo changes that form different substances. The particles in the original substance are arranged in different ways to form the particles of the new substance. As a result, the new substance has its own unique set of properties that differ from the original substance. Some examples of chemical properties are flammability and reactivity.

When the two nails that looked alike were left outside, only one had a change that indicated that a new substance had formed. Nail 1 rusted, while nail 2 did not rust. The rust is made of particles that are different from the particles in nail 1. The particles that make up nail 2 did not change into a new substance. Therefore, the two nails left outside are not made of the same substance.

EVIDENCE NOTEBOOK

6. How might properties of a substance help you explain what happened when sulfuric acid was mixed with powdered sugar? Record your evidence.

Compare Properties of Matter

Different substances may have some properties that are the same, but not all of their properties will be the same. You may need evidence about several different properties to determine whether the two substances are the same.

7. Use the information in the table to calculate the density of each sample, and enter it in the table. Then compare the properties of these two samples.

	Sample A	Sample B
Color	colorless	colorless
Odor	odorless	odorless
Boiling Point	100 °C	100 °C
Freezing Point	0 °C	75 °C
Mass	5.5 g	10.4 g
Volume	5.5 mL	7.0 mL
Density = $\frac{mass}{volume}$	_____ $\frac{g}{mL}$	_____ $\frac{g}{mL}$

8. Using the data in the table for color, odor, and boiling point, circle the correct words to complete each statement.

The colors of Sample A and Sample B are the same / different.

The odors of Sample A and Sample B are the same / different.

The boiling points of Sample A and Sample B are the same / different.

9. Now use the data in the table for freezing point and density. Circle the correct words to complete each statement.

The freezing points of Sample A and Sample B are the same / different.

The densities of Sample A and Sample B are the same / different.

10. Based on all the data from the table, are these two samples the same substance? Explain why it is important to look at several properties before drawing a conclusion.

Comparing Physical Changes and Chemical Reactions

Changes in Matter

Changes to substances take place all around you every day. Changes such as water freezing or metal being hammered into a thinner sheet do not alter the identity of the substance. Changes such as milk spoiling or silver tarnishing do change the identity of substances.

11. Discuss Explain in your own words what changes you see taking place in the logs burning in the fireplace.

Physical Changes

When a physical change takes place, the identity of a substance remains the same after the physical change. The particles that make up the substance are the same before and after the physical change. So, physical changes do not change the substance into something different. Physical changes only change the appearance of the substance.

This wood is being cut with a saw.

Explore ONLINE!

Think about the following changes. Ice is a solid. When ice melts, it is liquid water. If liquid water boils, it becomes water vapor, a gas. Whether the water is a solid, liquid, or gas, it is the same substance. There is no change to the identity of the water molecules. The physical changes do not change water into a new substance.

12. The photo shows wood undergoing a physical change. Compare the cut wood to the original piece of wood. Write *the same* or *different* to complete each sentence.

After cutting, the size and shape of the wood are _____. The smaller pieces of wood are _____ substance as the original larger piece of wood. The smaller pieces of wood are made of _____ particles as the original larger piece of wood. The sawdust has _____ identity as the wood.

13. Why doesn't a change in a physical property change the identity of the substance? Explain in terms of the particles of a substance and give an example that is not water or wood.

Chemical Reactions

When substances are mixed together, a chemical change may or may not take place. When a chemical change does take place, the original substance changes into a different substance with different properties.

Explore
ONLINE!

Watch what happens when baking soda is added to vinegar.

A student measures baking soda into a balloon, attaches the balloon to the top of a flask containing vinegar, and empties the baking soda into the flask.

14. Observe what happens in the flask as the baking soda is added to the vinegar. Why do you think the balloon inflates?

15. What happens when the baking soda and vinegar are mixed? Circle the correct words to complete the explanation.

When these two substances are mixed, a gas / liquid forms.

The baking soda and vinegar react with each other and change state / form a new substance.

A chemical reaction changes the identity of a substance. A **chemical reaction** is the process in which the building blocks of matter—atoms—are rearranged to produce different substances. The original substance or substances in a chemical reaction are called **reactants.** The substance or substances that form in a chemical reaction are called **products.** During a chemical reaction, the same atoms that make up the original substance or substances regroup into different particles to form new substances. The new particles could be atoms, molecules, or subunits of extended structures.

During a chemical reaction, all the atoms present in the reactants will also be present in the product, but they are rearranged into new substances. Chemical reactions generally follow defined patterns each and every time they occur. Under the same conditions, reactants will always form the same products in a chemical reaction.

16. Write chemical reaction or physical change to label each photo.

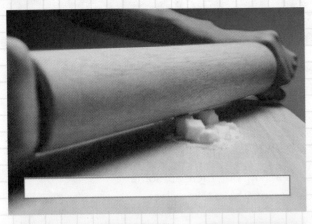

| |

chemical reaction

| |

| |

Analyze a Change in Matter

17. Look at the photo. How have the properties of the original material of the bucket changed? Circle all that apply.

   A. A chemical reaction has formed a new substance.

   B. The metal has reacted with air to form rust.

   C. The metal has changed to a different state.

   D. Rust has different properties than the metal.

18. How do you think the chemical reaction has affected how the bucket can be used?

_____

_____

_____

_____

19. Engineer It | Collaborate You have been asked to design a pipe system to deliver water. What criteria might you need to consider when choosing materials to use? Work together with a partner to develop a list. Choose one or two items from your list to incorporate into a short presentation for the class.

_____

_____

Analyzing Substances Before and After a Change

In a chemical reaction, the atoms of the reactants are rearranged to form new products. The products are different from the reactants and they have different properties. A change in properties is evidence of a chemical reaction.

Signs of a Possible Chemical Reaction

You cannot always see new substances form in a chemical reaction. But, there are some signs that you can observe to indicate that a chemical reaction may have taken place.

20. Each photo shows an indication that a chemical reaction may have taken place. Write the letter to label each photo.

A. Energy is released.
B. A precipitate forms.
C. The color changes.
D. A gas appears.
E. The odor changes.

C

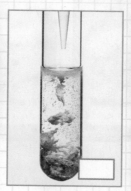

Some observations that are signs of a chemical reaction include a change in color, a change in odor, the appearance of a gas, energy being released as light or heat, and formation of a precipitate. A precipitate is a solid that is produced as a result of a chemical reaction in a solution.

Most of these changes could also happen in ways that are not the result of a chemical reaction. The appearance of bubbles can indicate formation of a new gas, but bubbles also form when water boils. The only way to know for sure whether a chemical reaction has taken place is to perform more testing.

Evidence of a Chemical Reaction

To determine whether a chemical reaction has taken place, you can test the properties of the substances both before the change and after the change. The products of a chemical reaction are different substances than the reactants and will have different properties. These different properties can help identify the products.

EVIDENCE NOTEBOOK

21. How might knowing the indicators of a chemical reaction help you explain what happened when the sulfuric acid was mixed with powdered sugar? How does this relate to the rearrangement of atoms that occurs in a chemical reaction? Record your evidence.

Hands-On Lab
Observe Substances Before and After a Change

You will mix substances together, and then determine whether a chemical reaction has taken place.

Procedure and Analysis

STEP 1 In bag 1, add 1 level spoonful of baking soda and 1 level spoonful of powdered sugar. Record observations in the table.

STEP 2 In bag 2, add 1 level spoonful of baking soda and 1 level spoonful of road salt. Record observations in the table.

STEP 3 Add 10 mL of water to each of the small containers.

STEP 4 Carefully place a container of water into each bag. Do not spill the water. Zip each bag closed with little air in it.

STEP 5 Tip the container over in bag 1. Observe what happens and record observations in the table. Repeat for bag 2.

	Observations
Bag 1: baking soda + powdered sugar	
Bag 2: baking soda + road salt	
Bag 1: baking soda + powdered sugar + water	
Bag 2: baking soda + road salt + water	

STEP 6 Do you think a chemical reaction occurred in the bag with baking soda and powdered sugar and water? in the bag with baking soda and road salt and water? Give evidence to support your answers.

22. Which observations would be evidence of a chemical reaction? Circle all that apply.

    A. A substance dissolved.

    B. A precipitate formed.

    C. A substance changed state.

    D. A gas was produced.

23. Draw lines to match each list of observations with the conclusion that it indicates.

• a gas was produced • the color changed
• the sample melted • the sample dissolved in water
• bubbles formed • the temperature climbed

does not indicate a chemical reaction
may indicate a chemical reaction
definite evidence of a chemical reaction

Observations such as the formation of a precipitate, the production of light or heat, or a change in color suggest that a chemical reaction has taken place, but these indications are not conclusive. Definite evidence for a chemical reaction requires proof that at least one new substance is present after the change. The presence of a new substance is determined by comparing the physical properties and chemical properties of the substances before and after the change.

Analyze Physical Changes and Chemical Reactions

24. Circle the correct terms to complete each sentence.

    A. The burning of the candle wick shows a
       chemical reaction / physical change.

    B. The melting of the wax shows a
       chemical reaction / physical change.

    C. The change of state / generation of light and heat
       indicates a chemical reaction may be occurring.

25. Language SmArts Create a labeled diagram using your own pictures and words to show and explain the processes that are going on as a candle burns. Note any physical changes or chemical reactions that may be taking place. Make sure to illustrate and describe any indication that supports a claim of a chemical reaction.

Continue Your Exploration

Name: _____ Date: _____

Check out the path below or go online to choose one of the other paths shown.

| Chemistry and Engineering: Airbags | • Hands-On Labs ✋
• Chemical Reactions Are Essential for Life
• Propose Your Own Path | *Go online to choose one of these other paths.* |

Using Chemical Reactions in a Product

Chemical reactions take place all around us. One chemical reaction you hope you never need is the one that takes place in the airbags of cars. In the event of an accident, the airbag inflates very quickly and cushions the people in a car to protect them from serious injury. The airbag inflates because a chemical reaction happens quickly after a crash sensor is activated. The chemical reaction produces a large volume of gas that fills the airbag. The airbag is not meant to replace safety belts. It is an additional safety feature.

▶ *Explore ONLINE!*

The chemical reaction that inflates an airbag happens very quickly! The time it takes for the airbag to fully inflate is less than a second.

MarkÅ/age fotostock

Chemistry and Engineering: Airbags

Inside the airbag is a chemical called sodium azide, which is made up of sodium and nitrogen atoms. When the crash sensor is triggered, heat is sent to the sodium azide. The heat causes the sodium azide to undergo an explosive chemical reaction. The sodium azide molecules break apart and produce a large volume of nitrogen gas. This causes the airbag to inflate rapidly.

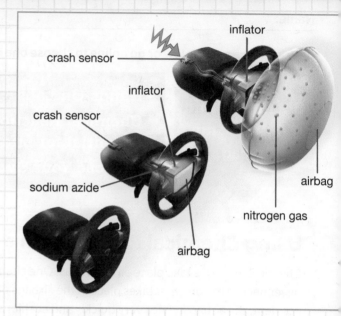

1. Which best describes how the chemical reaction that produces nitrogen gas inflates the airbag?

   A. The sodium azide quickly breaks apart.

   B. The sodium azide suddenly melts.

   C. The sodium azide rapidly forms a precipitate.

2. What indicates that a chemical reaction has taken place? Explain why the indicator would be a sign of a chemical reaction and not a sign of a physical change.

3. Chemical reactions are part of many different products. What are important considerations about a particular chemical reaction when it is used as part of the product design? Circle all that apply.

   A. the properties of product formed

   B. the properties of the reactants

   C. the cost of the reactants

   D. the safety of the chemical reaction

4. **Collaborate** Together with a partner, choose one of the topics below to discuss. Present your ideas to the class.

   • What sort of criteria are important for an airbag? What would need to be tested?

   • Can airbags be reused? Is it important to be able to reuse airbags? Why or why not?

   • Think about the problem for which the airbag was designed. Can you think of a different solution? Make a drawing/diagram to illustrate your idea.

   • What safety issues would need to be considered when designing airbags?

   • What environmental issues would need to be considered when designing airbags?

Can You Explain It?

Name: _____   **Date:** _____

What happens when sulfuric acid is added to powdered sugar?

Explore ONLINE!

EVIDENCE NOTEBOOK

Refer to the notes in your Evidence Notebook to help you construct an explanation for what you observed when sulfuric acid was added to powdered sugar.

1. State your claim. Make sure your claim fully explains what happens when these two substances are mixed.

2. Summarize the evidence you have gathered to support your claim and explain your reasoning.

Science Source

Checkpoints

Answer the following questions to check your understanding of the lesson.

3. Students were given a solid Sample A and made these observations. Write physical property or chemical property to indicate what kind of property is being tested.

   Sample A melted when heated to 52 °C. _____

   Sample A floated when dropped into water. _____

   Sample A burned when held in a flame. _____

4. A science class did an experiment in which two substances were mixed. After 15 minutes, everything looked the same, but the students noticed an odor coming from the experiment. What does this likely indicate?

   A. A liquid was formed.

   B. A temperature change occurred.

   C. A chemical reaction occurred.

   D. A physical change occurred.

Use the photo to answer Question 5.

5. Which of the following is the best evidence that a chemical change has taken place?

   A. The apple is smaller in size after cutting.

   B. The apple is turning brown.

   C. The apple has changed shape.

Use the photo to answer Questions 6 and 7.

6. Two metal samples are each placed in a beaker containing the same solution. What evidence indicates that a chemical reaction is taking place in one of the beakers? Circle all that apply.

   A. A gas is being given off.

   B. There is a change in color.

   C. The solution is clear and colorless.

   D. Bubbles are forming.

7. Based on what you observe in the beakers, which of the following statements is true?

   A. Chemical reactions can always be seen.

   B. The two samples of metal are different substances.

   C. Chemical reactions are unpredictable.

   D. New substances are formed in each beaker.

Interactive Review

Complete this section to review the main concepts of the lesson.

Physical properties and chemical properties are used to identify a substance.

A. Explain the difference between a physical property and a chemical property and give at least one example of each.

Physical changes do not form new substances but chemical reactions do.

B. Explain the changes that happen in a chemical reaction in terms of atoms.

The products of a chemical reaction have different properties than the reactants.

C. How can you gather evidence to determine whether a chemical reaction has taken place?

Chemical Equations

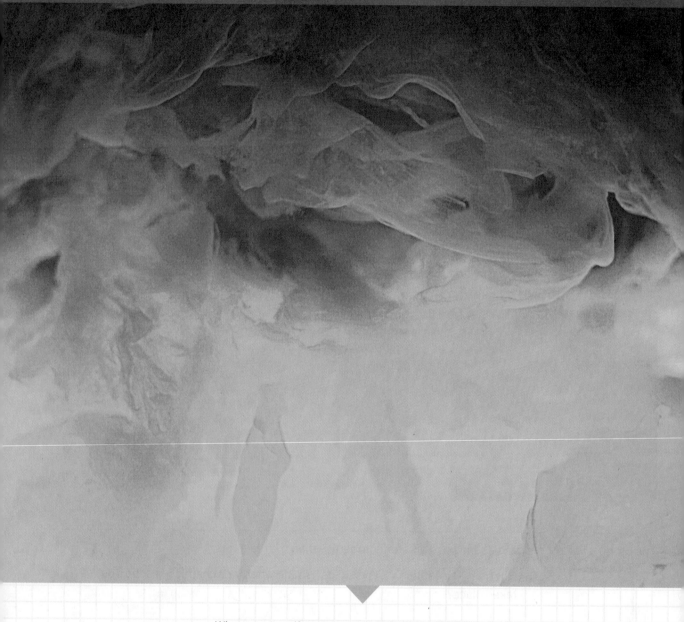

When copper sulfate reacts with ammonia, a precipitate forms and the solution color changes to deep blue.

By the end of this lesson . . .

you will be able to explain how chemical equations model chemical reactions and demonstrate the law of conservation of matter.

Go online to view the digital version of the Hands-On Lab for this lesson and to download additional lab resources.

CAN YOU EXPLAIN IT?

How does this chemical equation explain what happens when copper reacts with silver nitrate?

$$Cu + 2AgNO_3 \rightarrow Cu(NO_3)_2 + 2Ag$$

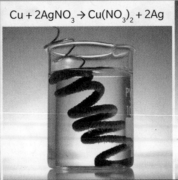

When a copper wire is placed in a solution of silver nitrate, silver metal and copper nitrate form.

Explore ONLINE!

1. Based on the photos, what do you think happens when copper reacts with silver nitrate?

2. What do you think the letters, numbers, and arrow represent in the chemical equation?

EVIDENCE NOTEBOOK As you explore the lesson, gather evidence to help you account for the matter that is rearranged in a chemical reaction.

Using Chemical Formulas

Students connected blocks together in three different combinations. They labeled each group with a code to describe how it is built.

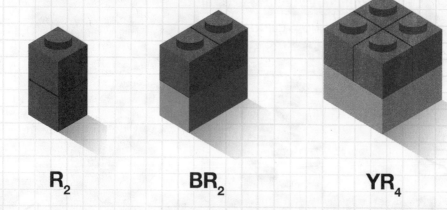

R_2 BR_2 YR_4

Each code represents the group of blocks above it.

3. Explain how the code describes each group of blocks in the images above.

Chemical Formulas

You and everything around you, including air, water, your phone, and your clothes, are made of chemical substances. These substances are made of the atoms of chemical elements combined with one another in different ways.

Think about the code used to show the combinations of blocks. How could a similar code be used to represent a chemical substance? A combination of chemical symbols and numbers that represents a single unit of a substance is called a **chemical formula**. For many substances, this single unit is a molecule. A molecule is a specific group of atoms held together by chemical bonds. In other substances, the single unit is part of a larger, repeating pattern of atoms. The chemical formula shows the exact atoms in each molecule or unit.

In any substance containing atoms of different elements, the atoms are always present in the same ratio. In other words, a chemical formula shows the relative numbers of atoms of each kind in a chemical compound.

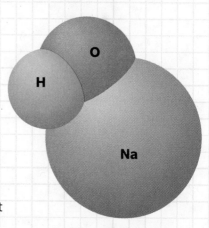

Sodium hydroxide (NaOH) is made up of a sodium atom (Na), an oxygen atom (O), and a hydrogen atom (H).

Water Molecule

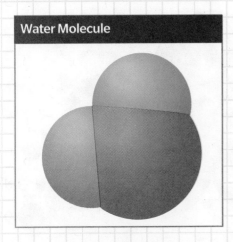

4. The chemical formula for water is H_2O. Explain how this chemical formula describes the model of a water molecule shown in this diagram.

A chemical formula uses **symbols of the** elements that make up the substance. A *subscript,* **a number below** and to the right of the symbol, shows how many atoms of **that element** there are. If there is no subscript, then one atom **of that element** is present.

Chemical Formula of Sulfuric Acid

A molecule of sulfuric acid is made up of 2 hydrogen atoms, 1 sulfur atom, and 4 oxygen atoms.

atom $\overset{}{H_2SO_4}$ subscript

5. Write the chemical **formula to identify** each model shown.

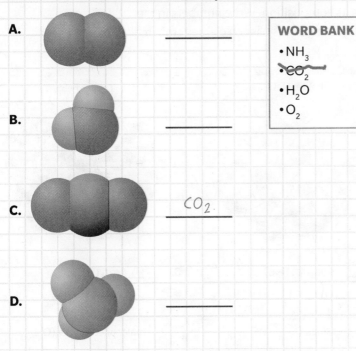

A. _____

B. _____

C. CO_2 _____

D. _____

WORD BANK
- NH_3
- CO_2
- H_2O
- O_2

Sometimes a formula **includes a group** of symbols in parentheses. This group in parentheses represents **atoms that are** held together as a group within the compound. Subscripts outside the **parentheses** show the number of groups there are. For example, the chemical formula $Al_2(SO_4)_3$ **describes** a compound that contains 2 aluminum atoms, 3 sulfur atoms, and 12 oxygen **atoms.**

6. How many atoms of **each element** are in the compound described by this chemical formula?

$$(CH_3)_2N$$

Each molecule of the **compound** has ___2___ atom(s) of carbon (C), _____ atom(s) of hydrogen (H), and _____ atom(s) of nitrogen (N).

7. The chemical formula below describes the model, but the subscript is missing. Write the subscript. Then write numbers to show how many atoms of each element are in the formula.

HNO ☐

The chemical formula shows there is (are):

_____ atom(s) of hydrogen

_____ atom(s) of nitrogen

_____ atom(s) of oxygen

H

N

O

Analyze the Chemical Formulas of Minerals

8. Minerals are natural substances that form as a result of processes in the rock cycle. Most minerals consist of repeating units of atoms or groups of atoms. The chemical formula given for each mineral describes its composition. Write numbers in the blanks below each photo to show the number of atoms of each element that make up a unit of the mineral.

hematite: Fe_2O_3

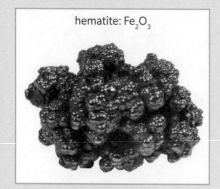

halite: NaCl

pyrite: FeS_2

A. __2__ iron (Fe),
    __3__ oxygen (O)

B. _____ sodium (Na),
    _____ chlorine (Cl)

C. _____ iron (Fe),
    _____ sulfur (S)

diamond: C

grossular: $Ca_3Al_2(SiO_4)_3$

malachite: $Cu_2CO_3(OH)_2$

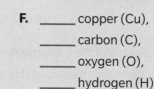

D. _____ carbon (C)

E. _____ calcium (Ca),
    _____ aluminum (Al),
    _____ silicon (Si),
    _____ oxygen (O)

F. _____ copper (Cu),
    _____ carbon (C),
    _____ oxygen (O),
    _____ hydrogen (H)

© Houghton Mifflin Harcourt • Image Credits: ©sakdinon/iStock/Getty Images Plus/Getty

Analyzing Chemical Equations

During a chemical reaction, new chemical substances form. Atoms grouped together in molecules or chemical units in the reactants rearrange and form different molecules or units in the products. The products of the chemical reaction have properties that are different from the reactants because the molecules that make up the products are different from those in the reactants.

The changes in these robots model the kinds of changes that happen in a chemical reaction.

9. Explain what is happening in the image. How are the changes in the robots like a chemical reaction?

10. **Draw** Make your own drawing to model reactants rearranging and forming new products.

Chemical Equations

Chemical formulas model chemical substances. A **chemical equation** uses chemical formulas to model what happens in a chemical reaction. It shows how the substances that are reacting change and form the products of the reaction. The way a chemical equation is written is similar to that of a mathematical equation.

In a chemical equation, one or more chemical formulas are shown, separated by addition signs. The formulas are followed by an arrow pointing to the right and then one or more different chemical formulas are shown. The formulas for the reactants are to the left of the arrow, and the formulas for the products are to the right.

11. Look at the chemical equation below. There is a number in the chemical equation that is not a subscript. What do you think the number 2 on the right side of the chemical equation represents?

$$H_2 + Cl_2 \rightarrow 2HCl$$

In a chemical equation, a *coefficient* is a number placed in front of a chemical formula to show how many molecules of the substance are represented in the chemical equation. In the reaction shown above, the coefficient of the HCl is 2, because two molecules of hydrogen chloride are formed in the reaction for every one molecule of H_2 and Cl_2.

The Electrolysis of Water

When an electric current passes through water, water breaks down into hydrogen and oxygen. The products of this reaction are not single atoms of hydrogen and oxygen, but molecules of hydrogen gas and oxygen gas. To model this reaction correctly, the chemical equation shows hydrogen and oxygen as gas molecules H_2 and O_2. The coefficients of the water and of the hydrogen gas are 2. Only one molecule of oxygen is produced, so no coefficient appears in front of the chemical formula for the oxygen gas.

$$2H_2O \longrightarrow 2H_2 + O_2$$

reactants   products

$$CH_4 + 2O_2 \rightarrow CO_2 + 2H_2O$$

coefficient   subscript

12. Circle the correct word to make each sentence true.

A. A chemical *equation / formula* shows both the reactants and the products of a chemical reaction.

B. The same *atoms / substances* are present on both sides of a chemical equation.

C. The arrow in a chemical equation points to the *products / reactants*.

Use a Model to Write a Chemical Equation

13. Write formulas in the boxes to show the chemical equation for this model of a chemical reaction.

Na₂S	H₂S
2NaCl	2HCl

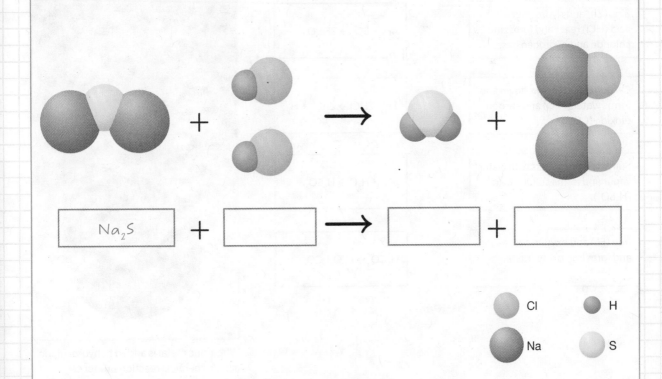

Na₂S + ☐ → ☐ + ☐

○ Cl   ● H

● Na   ○ S

Chemical Equations Model Chemical Reactions

During a chemical reaction, the reactants change into different substances, which are called the products. A chemical equation is a model that represents that change. Models help us learn about things that cannot be observed directly. The rearrangement of atoms that is happening in the chemical reaction cannot be directly observed. But the chemical equation helps to keep track of the rearrangment that is taking place.

A chemical equation shows that the same atoms are present before and after a reaction. Each side of the equation contains the same number and types of atoms. For example, think about the chemical equation for the burning of methane:

$$CH_4 + 2O_2 \rightarrow CO_2 + 2H_2O$$

This chemical equation models a chemical reaction. The chemical bonds between hydrogen and carbon and between oxygen atoms are broken. New chemical bonds form between carbon and oxygen and between hydrogen and oxygen.

The substances on one side of the arrow are different from the substances on the other side of the arrow. Atoms have recombined into new molecules, modeled by the chemical formulas.

The equation shows what happens to the reactants under a certain set of conditions. If an experiment is carried out under the same conditions that were used to determine the equation, the same reactants will always form the same products.

 14. Language SmArts Draw a line to match each description of a chemical reaction with the equation that models it.

Zinc (Zn) and hydrochloric acid (HCl) react and form zinc chloride and hydrogen gas.		$4Fe + 3O_2 \rightarrow 2Fe_2O_3$
Carbonic acid breaks down and forms water (H_2O) and carbon dioxide (CO_2).		$Zn + 2HCl \rightarrow ZnCl_2 + H_2$
Sulfur trioxide reacts with water vapor and forms sulfuric acid (H_2SO_4).		$SO_3 + H_2O \rightarrow H_2SO_4$
Iron (Fe) and oxygen gas react and form iron oxide (rust).		$H_2CO_3 \rightarrow H_2O + CO_2$

When zinc metal is added to hydrochloric acid, a chemical reaction produces hydrogen gas.

Hands-On Lab
Observe a Chemical Reaction

You will plan and carry out an investigation to observe what happens when acetic acid and baking soda are mixed. Acetic acid is a liquid ingredient in vinegar which gives vinegar its distinctive odor and taste.

Procedure and Analysis

STEP 1 Measure an amount of baking soda between 5–10 grams into the bag. Record the amount in the table.

STEP 2 Measure 30 mL of vinegar using the graduated cylinder. Pour the vinegar into the cup.

STEP 3 Place the bag into the pan. Place the cup of vinegar upright into the bag. Be careful not to spill the vinegar. Get as much air out of the bag as possible, and zip the bag closed.

STEP 4 Tip the cup over in the bag. Observe what happens, and record your observations in the table.

Vinegar/Baking Soda Experiment		
Baking soda (g)	Vinegar (mL)	Observations
	30	

STEP 5 The chemical equation for the reaction that you observed is:

sodium bicarbonate + acetic acid → sodium acetate + water + carbon dioxide
    (solid)   (liquid)   (solution)   (liquid)   (gas)

$$NaHCO_3 + C_2H_4O_2 \rightarrow NaC_2H_3O_2 + H_2O + CO_2$$

How can you use the chemical equation to explain what you observed when you added vinegar (acetic acid) to baking soda (sodium bicarbonate)? Use atoms in your explanation.

EVIDENCE NOTEBOOK

15. How does a chemical equation help to keep track of what happens in a chemical reaction? Record your evidence.

Identify a Chemical Equation

A solution of hydrogen peroxide can be used to kill germs on a small cut. Over time, though, the peroxide becomes less effective.

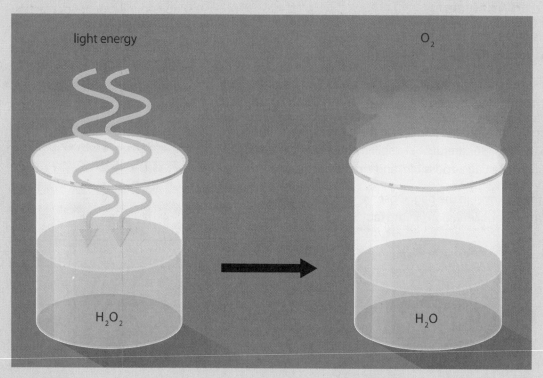

16. The image shows that hydrogen peroxide (H_2O_2) changes to oxygen gas and water. Which chemical equation models this reaction? Circle your answer.

A. $H_2O_2 \rightarrow H_2O$

B. $2H_2O_2 \rightarrow O_2 + 2H_2O$

C. $O_2 + 2H_2O \rightarrow 2H_2O_2$

17. Engineer It A packaging engineer is designing a container to hold hydrogen peroxide. The engineer knows that light speeds up the chemical reaction that changes hydrogen peroxide into oxygen and water. How might the engineer use that information when designing the container? Give an example.

_____

_____

_____

_____

_____

_____

_____

Modeling Chemical Reactions

Any change that produces a new substance, or substances, is a chemical reaction. Chemical reactions occur around you all of the time. Some reactions, such as a log burning in a campfire, occur quickly and are easy to observe. Some reactions, such as the reactions that cause a green banana to ripen over several days, are much slower. Other reactions are harder to observe, such as the formation of ozone in the atmosphere.

18. In some chemical reactions, such as photosynthesis, several different compounds take part in the reaction. How do you think that atoms present at the end of this kind of reaction compare to the atoms present at the beginning of the reaction? Explain.

In the green parts of trees, the chemical reaction photosynthesis uses energy from the sun to convert carbon dioxide and water into sugar and oxygen.

The Law of Conservation of Matter

Chemical reactions do not always produce a visible product. For example, one product of photosynthesis, oxygen, cannot be observed by looking at a leaf. Scientists have measured the amount of carbon dioxide and water that react during photosynthesis. When they compared the mass of reactants and the mass of oxygen and plant material produced, they confirmed that the reactants and the products have the same mass.

The **law of conservation of matter** states that matter cannot be created or destroyed in ordinary chemical or physical changes. During any ordinary chemical or physical change, the total mass of the substances involved in the change is the same before and after the change. The new substances formed during a chemical reaction are made up of exactly the same atoms as the atoms of substances that reacted. The same atoms are present before and after the reaction. Matter is conserved because atoms are conserved. In other words, because the same atoms are present before and after the reaction, the mass of the reactants is the same as the mass of the products.

19. How do you think a chemical equation shows that matter is being conserved?

Balanced Chemical Equations Model the Conservation of Matter

Because a chemical equation is a model of a chemical reaction, the equation must show that the number of atoms does not change during the reaction. A chemical equation is *balanced* when it has the same number of each type of atom on both sides of the equation.

The fact that chemical equations have the same number and types of atoms on both sides of the equation demonstrates the law of conservation of matter.

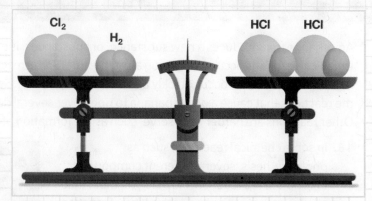

When H_2 and Cl_2 react and form 2HCl, the same number and types of atoms are in the reactants and in the products. The two sides balance.

Balanced Chemical Equations

Hydrogen and chlorine can combine and form hydrogen chloride, as shown in the picture and modeled by this chemical equation:

$$H_2 + Cl_2 \rightarrow 2HCl$$

20. If the reactants contain one chlorine molecule, do you know how many chlorine atoms will be in the product? Include conservation of matter in your explanation.

21. How do you think subscripts and coefficients help to tell whether a chemical equation is balanced?

You can determine whether a chemical equation is balanced by comparing the number of atoms of each element on both sides of the arrow. Every element must have the same number of atoms in the reactants and in the products for the equation to be balanced. As you count atoms in a chemical formula, remember that the subscript following a symbol tells you the number of atoms of that element present in one molecule or unit of a substance. If a coefficient is in front of a chemical formula, multiply the number of atoms of each element in that formula by the coefficient. For example, if an equation includes the term $2H_2O$, then 4 hydrogen atoms and 2 oxygen atoms are present.

The Conservation of Matter

A chemical equation is a model of what happens during a chemical reaction. It shows what reactants are being changed and what products form. Because every chemical reaction follows the law of conservation of matter, the chemical equation must demonstrate that law.

When a chemical equation is balanced, all matter on one side of the equation is also shown on the other side of the equation. The equation correctly models the chemical reaction by showing that matter is conserved.

Model a Balanced Chemical Equation

22. As methane burns, it reacts with oxygen and forms carbon dioxide and water. The balanced chemical equation below models this chemical reaction. Examine each molecule represented in the chemical equation. Write the numbers of each type of atom in the reactants and products. Compare the numbers when you are finished.

$$CH_4 + 2O_2 \rightarrow CO_2 + 2H_2O$$

Reactant side

Product side

_____ C atom(s)   _____ C atom(s)

_____ H atom(s)   _____ H atom(s)

_____ O atom(s)   _____ O atom(s)

23. **Act** Work with a group to demonstrate the law of conservation of matter by acting out this chemical equation:

$$CH_4 + 2O_2 \rightarrow CO_2 + 2H_2O$$

 EVIDENCE NOTEBOOK

24. How do balanced chemical equations help to account for everything that happens in a chemical reaction? Record your evidence.

25. Do the Math Compare the number of atoms of each element on both sides of each chemical equation. Write *balanced* or *not balanced* to describe each equation.

A. $C_2H_6 + 5O_2 \rightarrow 2CO_2 + 3H_2O$ _____

B. $3CO + Fe_2O_3 \rightarrow 2Fe + 3CO_2$ _____

C. $H_2SO_4 + 2NaOH \rightarrow Na_2SO_4 + 2H_2O$ _____

D. $2AgNO_3 + CaCl_2 \rightarrow 2AgCl + Ca(NO_3)_2$ _____

Evaluate a Chemical Equation

The photo shows that when a clear, colorless solution of lead nitrate is added to a clear, colorless solution of sodium iodide, a yellow solid, lead iodide, forms.

lead nitrate	+	sodium iodide	→	lead iodide	+	sodium nitrate
(solution)		(solution)		(solid)		(solution)
$Pb(NO_3)_2$	+	NaI	→	PbI_2	+	$NaNO_3$

26. Explain why the equation shown is not a balanced equation. Include conservation of matter in your explanation.

_____

_____

_____

_____

_____

_____

_____

27. A student proposed that the balanced chemical equation for this reaction is:

$$Pb(NO_3)_2 + 2NaI \rightarrow PbI_2 + 2NaNO_3$$

Determine whether this is a correctly balanced equation and give evidence for your conclusion.

_____

_____

_____

_____

_____

_____

_____

_____

Continue Your Exploration

Name: **Date:**

Check out the path below or go online to choose one of the other paths shown.

| Balancing a Chemical Equation | • Hands-On Labs ✋
 • Chemistry in the Kitchen
 • Propose Your Own Path | *Go online to choose one of these other paths.* |

If you know the reactants and the products of a chemical reaction, you can write a balanced chemical equation. You can model balancing a chemical reaction by using parts of an object that combine to form a complete object.

As in a balanced chemical equation, all of the parts on the left are shown in the bike on the right.

1. To build a bicycle, you need to start with the number of each part needed for the finished bike. A word description for constructing a bike could be written as:

frame + wheels + seat + pedals → bicycle

With a partner, write a "balanced equation" for a bicycle. Use F, W, S, and P as symbols for the "reactants." Use subscripts and coefficients to balance the bicycle equation. Include the formula for the finished bike.

Continue Your Exploration

To balance a chemical equation, change the coefficients to balance each type of atom. Subscripts are part of the chemical formula and cannot be changed. Here is an example.

$$C + O_2 \longrightarrow CO$$

C = 1   O = 2   C = 1 O = 1

$$2C + O_2 \longrightarrow 2CO$$

C = 2   O = 2   C = 2 O = 2

Count the atoms in the reactants and in the product. There are more oxygen atoms in the reactants than in the product. There are two oxygen atoms in the reactants, so you need two oxygen atoms in the product.

In order to have two oxygen atoms in the product, place a coefficient 2 in front of CO. Now the oxygen atoms balance, but the carbon atoms do not. Placing the coefficient 2 in front of the C reactant balances the equation.

2. Count the atoms of each element in the reactants and product in the unbalanced chemical equation. Write the numbers in the blanks below the model.

$$H_2 + O_2 \longrightarrow H_2O$$

H = _____ O = _____ → H = _____ O = _____

3. To balance the number of each type of atom, place coefficients in front of the appropriate chemical formulas. Then sketch the products and reactants, showing the correct number of molecules of each. Write the number of hydrogen and oxygen atoms in the reactants and products for the balanced reaction.

_____ H_2 + _____ O_2 → _____ H_2O

H = _____ O = _____ → H = _____ O = _____

4. **Collaborate** Work with a partner. Choose one of the unbalanced chemical equations shown. Find the coefficients needed to balance the equation and model the balanced equation by sketching the products and reactants. Present your sketch to the class and explain how it shows the balanced chemical equation.

$$Al + O_2 \rightarrow Al_2O_3$$

$$Na + H_2O \rightarrow NaOH + H_2$$

Can You Explain It?

Name: _____   **Date:** _____

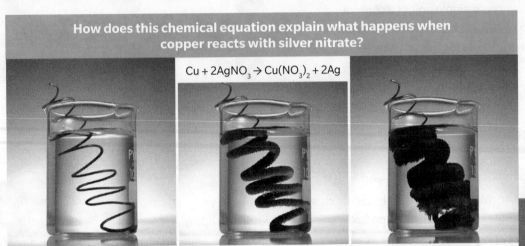

How does this chemical equation explain what happens when copper reacts with silver nitrate?

$$Cu + 2AgNO_3 \rightarrow Cu(NO_3)_2 + 2Ag$$

Explore ONLINE!

EVIDENCE NOTEBOOK

Refer to the notes in your Evidence Notebook to help you construct an explanation for the solid that forms when a copper wire is placed in a silver nitrate solution.

1. State your claim. Make sure your claim fully describes how the chemical equation explains what happens when copper reacts with silver nitrate.

2. Summarize the evidence you have gathered to support your claim and explain your reasoning.

Checkpoints

Answer the following questions to check your understanding of the lesson.

Use the model to answer Question 3.

3. This model shows a single unit of a compound containing several elements. Which of these is the chemical formula for the substance?

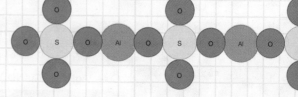

A. Al_2SO_4

B. $Al_2(SO_3)_4$

C. $Al_2(SO_4)_3$

D. $(AlO)_2(SO_4)_3$

Use the photo to answer Questions 4 and 5.

4. Zinc and hydrochloric acid are combined in a test tube. What can you conclude about the chemical reaction taking place? Circle all that apply.

A. The mass of the products is exactly the same as the mass of the reactants.

B. One new product formed is a gas.

C. Molecules are changing into different molecules.

D. Atoms are changing into different atoms.

5. The photo shows the reaction between zinc and hydrochloric acid that forms zinc chloride and hydrogen gas. Which of these is a correctly balanced equation that models the reaction?

A. $Zn + HCl \rightarrow ZnCl_2 + H_2$

B. $Zn + 2HCl \rightarrow ZnCl_2 + 2H_2$

C. $Zn + 2HCl \rightarrow ZnCl_2 + H_2$

D. $Zn + 4HCl \rightarrow ZnCl_2 + 2H_2$

6. What is shown by this balanced chemical equation? Circle all that apply.

$$H_2 + Cl_2 \rightarrow 2HCl$$

A. The atoms in the original substances regroup and form a different substance.

B. The product is a new substance made up of different atoms than the reactants.

C. The total number of atoms changes in the reaction.

D. The same atoms are present before and after the reaction.

E. Matter is conserved.

7. How many oxygen (O) atoms are involved in this chemical reaction?

$$2Fe(OH)_3 \rightarrow Fe_2O_3 + 3H_2O$$

A. 2

B. 3

C. 6

D. 12

Interactive Review

Complete this section to review the main concepts of the lesson.

A chemical formula is a model of a molecule or unit of a substance.

A. What information about a molecule can you determine from its chemical formula?

A chemical equation models what happens in a chemical reaction. It shows how the substances that are reacting change and form the products of the reaction.

B. Explain how a chemical equation shows that the reactants change and form the products.

The law of conservation of matter states that matter is not created or destroyed in ordinary chemical or physical changes.

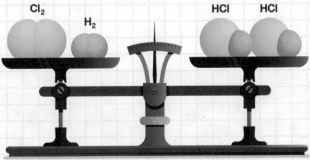

C. How does a balanced chemical equation show that a chemical reaction obeys the law of conservation of matter?

Thermal Energy and Chemical Processes

As the chemical reactions of the bonfire proceed, the air around the fire becomes hot.

By the end of this lesson . . .

you will be able to design, construct, and test a device that uses a chemical process to transfer thermal energy.

Go online to view the digital version of
the Hands-On Lab for this lesson and to
download additional lab resources.

CAN YOU EXPLAIN IT?

How can a device warm food without using fire or electricity?

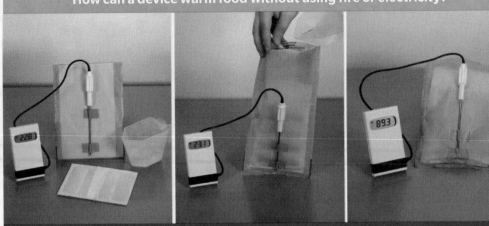

These photos show a digital thermometer measuring the temperature of a flameless heater.
Flameless heaters produce energy for cooking without flames or electricity. This heater
contains a mixture of iron and magnesium. Once water is added to the heater, the heater
begins to warm quickly. A bag of food can be warmed by putting it inside the heater.

Explore
ONLINE!

1. Observe the photos. What could be occurring inside the device to release thermal
   energy for cooking?

EVIDENCE NOTEBOOK As you explore the lesson, gather evidence to help
explain how a device could warm food without using fire or electricity.

Exploring Systems and Energy Flow

When you shoot a basketball, kinetic energy from your hand is transferred to the ball. Thermal energy can also be transferred between objects. Think about what happens when you touch a warm pan. How do you know that the pan is warm? Thermal energy from the pan is transferred to your hand. You experience this energy transfer as a feeling of warmth.

2. The hot metal objects in the photo cool quickly and soon stop glowing. What happens to the energy as the metal parts cool?

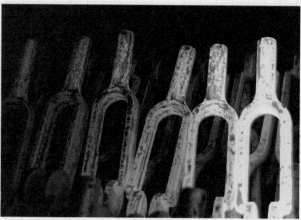

After each piece of metal is removed from the furnace, it begins to cool and glow less brightly.

Energy Flow in Systems

A system is a set of interacting parts. Systems can include matter, energy, and information. By grouping a set of related parts or events into a system, scientists and engineers can study how matter and energy behave.

A system can have inputs (things that enter the system) and outputs (things that leave the system). Inputs and outputs can be matter, energy, or information. New matter or energy cannot be created or destroyed. Instead, matter and energy can only be transformed into new forms or be introduced from outside the system. To accurately model a system, you must understand the inputs and outputs of that system. You also have to understand the flow of matter, energy, and information through the system.

For example, an automobile engine uses energy to make a car move. The inputs of the system are gasoline and air. When gasoline and air enter the engine system, they react with one another. The chemical energy of the gasoline-air reaction is converted into thermal energy and then mechanical energy by the engine. The mechanical energy is an output of the engine system and is used to move a car. By tracing the flow of energy, we can understand how the system functions.

3. Look at the temperatures of the water, the metal object, and the air to explain the flow of thermal energy in this system. What do the arrows show?

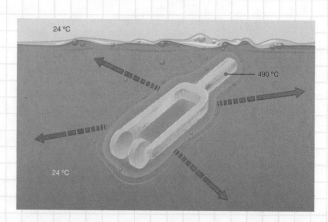

24 °C

490 °C

24 °C

4. Why do the contents of the ice chest in the photo stay cold even though the air around the chest is warm?

   A. Thermal energy flows from the ice to the drink containers.

   B. Thermal energy flows from the drink containers to the ice chest.

   C. The ice chest accelerates the flow of thermal energy to the environment.

   D. The ice chest slows the flow of thermal energy from the environment to the ice and drinks.

The ice chest and its contents can be studied as a system.

Types of Energy Transfer

All matter is made up of tiny particles that are in constant motion. The particles of matter in an object move faster when the object is warm than when the object is cold. When thermal energy flows from one object to another, it always flows from the warmer object to the cooler object. As a result, the motion of the particles in the two objects changes. Thermal energy can be transferred between objects in several different ways.

Conduction, convection, and radiation are ways that thermal energy is transferred. In conduction, thermal energy is transferred as particles bump into one another. Warmer particles move more rapidly, and as they bump into cooler particles, energy is transferred to the cooler particles. In convection, thermal energy is transferred through matter that flows. Cold particles sink and force warm particles to rise. This movement causes thermal energy to be transferred to different areas of a liquid or gas. In radiation, energy is transferred by light or other electromagnetic radiation. This radiation travels until it reaches a particle. Radiation is then absorbed by the particle and transformed into thermal energy. Radiation can travel through space, where there is no matter.

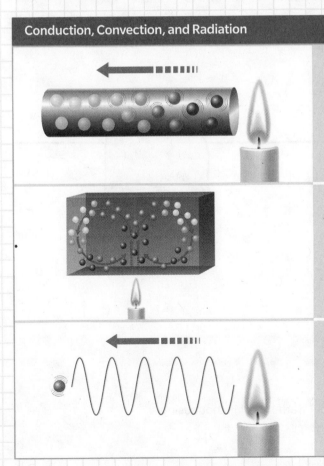

Conduction, Convection, and Radiation

Conduction Thermal energy is transferred between particles through conduction. In this example, the candle is warming one end of the metal bar. The particles in the metal bar start to move faster as they gain more thermal energy. As the particles move faster, they bump into each other and transfer thermal energy through the metal rod.

Convection Thermal energy is transferred throughout liquids and gases through convection. In this example, the candle is heating the box. As air in the box warms, the air particles begin to move faster, and the air becomes less dense. The colder, denser air sinks and pushes up the warmer air. This movement transfers thermal energy through liquids and gases.

Radiation Radiation is the transfer of energy through electromagnetic waves. In this example, the candle produces infrared radiation. This radiation travels through empty space until it hits a particle. The particle then absorbs this radiation, and the radiation is converted into thermal energy. This process is how thermal energy is transferred through space.

5. The airless vacuum of outer space is extremely cold, but objects in space do not cool nearly as fast as you might expect. Which statement most likely explains this?

  A. Objects in space are already cold, so they do not transfer thermal energy.

  B. There is no matter in space to transfer thermal energy to by conduction or convection.

  C. Convection carries thermal energy from the sun to objects in space and keeps them warm.

  D. Radiation does not occur in space because of the lack of air.

Specially designed suits protect astronauts from the cold and airless space around them.

Model Energy Movement

If you want to understand a device that uses energy, it is important to know how energy will move through the device and any system that the device could be part of. You can map energy flows with arrows to visualize how energy flows through any system.

6. Show how thermal energy would flow through this system. Draw arrows to show the direction of thermal energy flow.

EVIDENCE NOTEBOOK

  7. How would the energy flow in a device that warms food without using a flame or electricity? Record your evidence.

156 Unit 3 Chemical Processes and Equations

Analyzing Energy in Chemical Processes

Thermal energy is not the only form of energy. Many systems produce thermal energy when a different form of energy is transformed into thermal energy. For example, some of the radiant energy of sunlight is changed into thermal energy in the particles of matter that make up the atmosphere. Other forms of energy that can be changed into thermal energy include chemical, kinetic, and electrical energy.

Explore ONLINE!

Energy Changes in a Hand Warmer

When a small tab in this hand warmer is bent, the sodium acetate inside the hand warmer starts to form crystals. As the crystals form, the sodium acetate releases thermal energy.

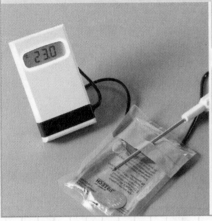

8. Which type of energy is likely changed into thermal energy in this hand warmer?

   A. electromagnetic energy

   B. electrical energy

   C. chemical energy

   D. kinetic energy

Energy and Chemical Processes

One way that energy can be transformed is through chemical processes. Chemical processes include chemical reactions in which the identity of matter changes, and physical changes such as a change of state or the dissolution of a solid in a liquid. Chemical processes can transform the energy stored in chemical bonds or in the arrangement of molecules into thermal energy.

Most chemical processes involve a change in energy. Some processes, such as melting ice cubes, absorb thermal energy. Other processes, like the burning of paper, release thermal energy. The change in thermal energy will depend on the change in the energy stored in the chemical bonds or molecular structures. If a large amount of a solid melts, the amount of thermal energy absorbed will be larger than if a small amount of the solid melts.

Explore ONLINE!

The temperature of the steel wool increased from 20.6 °C to 26.5 °C when the iron in the steel wool rusted. Vinegar was used to accelerate this normally slow reaction.

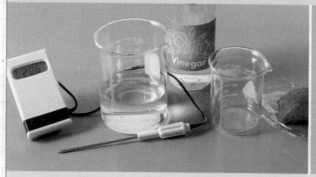

The temperature of this solution dropped from −0.8 °C to −8.0 °C when the rock salt was dissolved in the water.

9. Draw a line connecting the chemical processes shown in the photos to the change in thermal energy that occurs during the process.

iron rusting	absorbs thermal energy
salt dissolving in water	releases thermal energy

Rates of Energy Transformation

Chemical processes do not all transform energy at the same rate. The rate of energy transformation depends on the type of chemical process. A fire releases thermal energy very quickly. Inside a muscle, a similar chemical reaction releases the energy that the muscle needs to move. This process transforms chemical energy into thermal energy at a slower rate than a fire does. The rate of energy transformation also depends on how quickly a chemical process occurs. A candle burning quickly will release energy faster than a candle that is barely burning. A hamster running on a wheel will release energy faster than a sleeping hamster. Both the chemical process and the rate of the chemical process affect how quickly energy is transformed in a given situation.

EVIDENCE NOTEBOOK

10. How might the rates of energy transformation affect how the flameless heater is able to warm objects? Record your evidence.

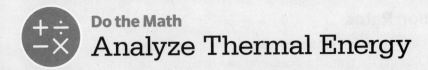

Do the Math
Analyze Thermal Energy

Two things must be considered when you use a chemical process to release thermal energy. One factor is the amount of chemical energy that a process can transform into thermal energy. This can be measured as the number of joules of energy produced by one unit of reactant. The second factor to consider is how quickly the process releases energy. This rate is the number of units of reactants that react per second.

This table shows the amount of energy released when one unit of each substance combines with oxygen in a combustion reaction. Combustion reactions usually involve a fire or explosion.

Reactant	kJ/unit Released in combustion
hydrogen	286
ethanol	1,371
propane	2,219

11. Which reactant releases the most energy when a single unit is combusted?

12. In each sentence, choose the number that represents the correct answer.

   A. Under certain conditions, 6 units of hydrogen will burn in 1 second. This process releases energy at a rate of 286 / 572 / 1,716 kJ per second.

   B. Under the same conditions, 1 unit of ethanol will burn in 1 second. This process releases energy at a rate of 686 / 1,371 / 8,226 kJ per second.

   C. Under these conditions, hydrogen / ethanol will release more energy in 1 second.

13. Which of the following factors affect how quickly burning hydrogen, ethanol, and propane will release energy? Choose all that apply.

   A. the reactant burned

   B. the number of reactants in the chemical process

   C. the location of the chemical process

   D. the amount of reactant burned per second

Factors That Affect Reaction Rates

In order to use a chemical process to control the flow of thermal energy, you must understand how the process works. Knowing the type of process and how to control the rate at which it takes place allows you to adjust the rate of the process. There are many factors that control the rates of chemical processes. The diagrams below show some important factors that can be used control the rates of chemical reactions.

Chemical Reaction Rate Variables

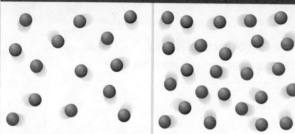 

Concentration Increasing the concentration of reactants can cause a reaction to occur faster. This happens because increasing the concentration means that the reactants come into contact more often.

Temperature Increasing temperature can cause the reaction to occur faster. When particles have more energy, they move faster. The faster particles are moving, the more often they will come into contact with each other.

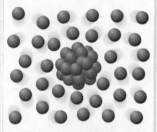 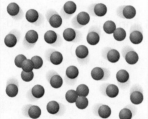  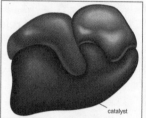

Surface Area Increasing the surface area of a solid reactant increases the reaction rate because the increased surface area allows more particles of the other reactants to collide with the particles of the solid.

Catalysts Catalysts are materials that increase the rate of a chemical reaction by bringing together reactants. The catalyst itself is not used up or changed very much.

Chemical reactions are only one type of chemical process. The rates of other chemical processes, such as dissolution or state changes, can be affected by some of these same factors. For instance, temperature can affect how quickly a solid dissolves in a liquid. The surface area of a solid can affect how quickly the solid changes state to a liquid. Catalysts may not have any effect on many chemical processes. There are many different types of chemical processes. Not all chemical processes will be affected in the same way by these factors. Some chemical processes may be affected by other factors as well.

14. Which statement correctly explains how increasing the reaction rate affects the thermal energy of a chemical reaction?

   A. It increases the total amount of energy absorbed or released.

   B. It decreases the total amount of energy absorbed or released.

   C. It increases the rate at which energy is transformed, but not the amount of energy of the reaction.

   D. It increases the total amount of energy transformed, but not the rate at which energy is transformed.

Analyze a Chemical Process

Ammonium chloride is a white crystalline compound. When crystals of ammonium chloride are mixed with water, they dissolve to form a solution. As the crystals dissolve, the solution absorbs thermal energy. The temperature of the solution will decrease. The temperature of the solution can decrease enough to cause water on the outside of the container to freeze.

15. Make a sketch that shows how thermal and chemical energy interact in the system made up of water and ammonium chloride.

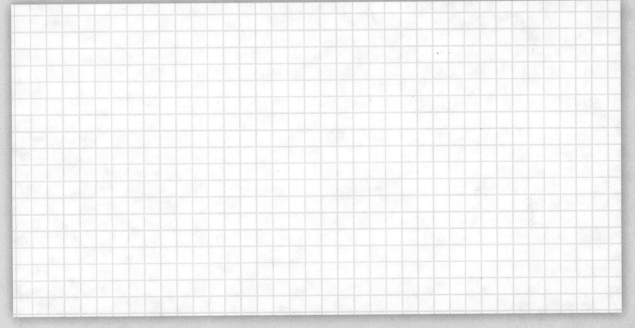

16. Describe the flow of energy shown in your sketch of the water and ammonium chloride system.

_____

_____

_____

_____

_____

_____

_____

Designing a Cold Pack

When you twist an ankle or sprain your wrist, an ice pack can help reduce the swelling and pain from the injury. If you are hiking in the wilderness or playing on a ball field, ice might not be easy to find. In that case, how could you treat your hurt ankle? A chemical cold pack might be just what you need. You can carry the cold pack with you. You do not need a cooler or ice to store it. When you do need a cold pack, you just start the chemical process inside the sealed package. Within a few seconds, the pack will begin to cool.

To keep swelling down, treat a sprained ankle as soon as possible.

17. Which of the following would be included in the criteria for a chemical cold pack that you could take along on a hike? Choose all that apply.

A. small and easy to carry

B. becomes cold quickly when activated

C. flexible enough to form around injured area

D. packaging that transfers thermal energy well

Hands-On Lab
Choose a Chemical Process

You will test different chemical processes that might be used in a chemical cold pack. You will calculate the temperature changes that occur. You will also make observations about how each chemical process might behave in a cold pack.

To design a chemical cold pack, you must determine what characteristics a process should have in order to be a solution to your engineering problem. Think about the criteria and constraints of the problem as you test each process. The cold pack must get cold as a result of a chemical process. The process must occur rapidly so that the cold pack is available when needed.

MATERIALS
- ammonium chloride
- baking soda
- balance
- beakers, 500 mL, (4)
- calcium chloride
- graduated cylinders, 100 mL (2)
- paper towels
- steel wool, fine
- stirrers
- thermometer
- vinegar
- water

Procedure

STEP 1 Choose a pair of liquid and solid components from Table 1 at the bottom of the page. Measure 100 mL of the liquid component into a beaker. Measure the temperature of the liquid. Record your measurement in Table 2 on the next page.

STEP 2 Add 10 grams of the solid component to the beaker. Stir the mixture. Record any changes that you observe in Table 1 at the bottom of the page.

STEP 3 After 2 minutes, measure the temperature of the liquid. Record your measurement in Table 2 on the next page.

STEP 4 Repeat Steps 1–3 with each of the other combinations of materials. Note any observations that might affect the usefulness of each combination for the cold pack.

Table 1		
Liquid component	Solid component	Observations
vinegar	steel wool	
vinegar	baking soda	
water	calcium chloride	
water	ammonium chloride	

Analysis

STEP 5 Calculate the temperature change that takes place during each chemical process by subtracting the initial temperature from the final temperature. Record your answers in Table 2.

		Table 2		
Liquid component	Solid component	Starting temperature (°C)	Ending temperature (°C)	Temperature change (°C)
vinegar	steel wool			
vinegar	baking soda			
water	calcium chloride			
water	ammonium chloride			

STEP 6 Which chemical processes absorbed thermal energy? Select all that apply.

   A. vinegar/steel wool

   B. vinegar/baking soda

   C. water/calcium chloride

   D. water/ammonium chloride

STEP 7 Which process would you choose to use for your instant cold pack? Include an explanation of the flow of energy in your answer.

Design a Container

After you determine the best chemical process to use for the cold pack, you will design the cold pack itself. For the cold pack to be useful, it must be ready to become cold when you need it. However, the materials cannot mix too soon because the process cannot be repeated. You must design a way to keep the two substances apart until it is time to use the cold pack. Your design should be one package that is able to keep the two solutions separate so that they do not accidentally mix. Your design should also have a way to mix the two solutions easily so that you can use the cold pack when you need it.

18. What criteria would apply to the packaging or container in order to make the product useful? Select all that apply.

    A. flexible

    B. brightly colored

    C. keeps components separate during storage

    D. allows easy mixing when needed

19. **Draw** Make a sketch of a possible design for the device.

20. Explain your sketch and how the chemicals would be separated in your device. How could they be combined easily when needed?

21. Draw Make a sketch of the outside of your device. You may design a name and logo for your device if you like.

Choose a Material

When you choose materials for your device, you must consider how those materials could affect the function of the entire system. The device must be durable and able to form to an injured body part. It should also transfer thermal energy well. The table lists several different materials that you can consider. It shows the thermal conductivity value, which is the rate at which thermal energy passes through a material. Thermal conductivity is higher for materials that transfer thermal energy faster. Other factors may be as important, or even more important, than thermal conductivity.

Material	Thermal conductivity	Characteristics
Aluminum foil	205.00	Flexible, tears easily, hard
Glass	1.05	Rigid, strong, hard, breakable
Polythene	0.33	Flexible, strong, soft
Polystyrene	0.03	Rigid, easily punctured
Rubber	0.13	Flexible, very strong, soft

22. Which material would best meet the criteria and constraints of the cold pack? Explain your reasoning.

_____

_____

_____

_____

_____

_____

Continue Your Exploration

Name: _____   Date: _____

Check out the path below or go online to choose one of the other paths shown.

| People in Science | • **Hands-On Labs** 👆
• **Researching Chemical Processes**
• **Propose Your Own Path** | *Go online to choose one of these other paths.* |

Fritz Haber and Carl Bosch, Chemists

Ammonia is an important chemical in many industries and in the production of fertilizer. The Haber-Bosch process was developed to combat ammonia shortages. Fritz Haber, a German research chemist, developed the initial process. Haber's process reliably produced ammonia from nitrogen and hydrogen. Carl Bosch, a German industrial chemist, later engineered high-pressure equipment that could mass produce ammonia using Haber's initial process. Both men received Nobel Prizes for their work.

This process was the first industrial chemical process to use high pressure in chemical production. It combines nitrogen with hydrogen under very high pressures and temperatures. An iron catalyst allows the reaction to be carried out at a lower temperature than would otherwise be possible, but it is still very high (400 °C to 650 °C).

Fritz Haber was a chemical researcher and professor who developed the chemical reaction still used to make ammonia.

Carl Bosch used the engineering design process to develop equipment to produce ammonia on a large scale.

1. How does the Haber-Bosch process demonstrate the connection between science and engineering?

Continue Your Exploration

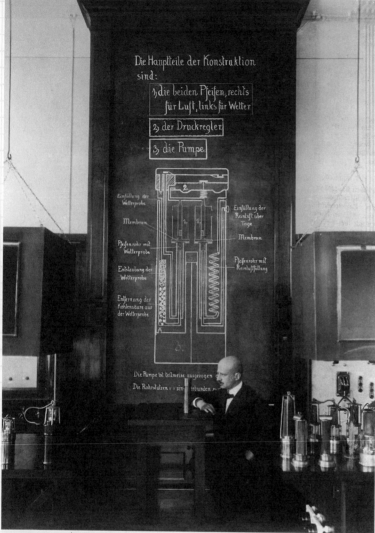

Die Hauptteile der Konstruktion
sind:

1) die beiden Pfeifen, rechts
für Luft, links für Wetter

2) der Druckregler

3) die Pumpe.

Einfüllung der
Wetterprobe

Membran

Pfeifenrohr mit
Wetterprobe

Entlaubung der
Wetterprobe

Entfernung der
Kohlensäure aus
der Wetterprobe

Einfüllung der
Reinluft über
Tage

Membran

Pfeifenrohr mit
Reinluffüllung

Die Pumpe ist teilweise ausgezogen

Die Rohrstutzen × × sind verbunden

A Haber-Bosch reactor uses catalysts and a series of pipes to combine nitrogen and hydrogen under high pressure.

2. Haber's original lab reaction worked on a very small scale. Once Bosch began to scale it up, it was apparent that the reaction produced large amounts of thermal energy. Which statement best explains why this might be a problem?

   A. Higher temperature increases the reaction rate.

   B. Too much thermal energy could damage equipment.

   C. Chemical processes work better when there is less thermal energy.

   D. Catalysts are never useful when the temperature is high.

3. High temperatures can damage equipment. Which of the following are ways to keep a Haber-Bosch reactor from getting too hot? Choose all that apply.

   A. Insulate the outside of the reaction vessel.

   B. Perform the reaction in a system that transfers thermal energy well.

   C. Surround the reaction vessel with flowing water that absorbs thermal energy.

   D. Remove some catalysts from the reaction.

4. **Collaborate** As a team, research ways that chemical industries control thermal energy involved in manufacturing processes. Prepare a report or presentation to describe one method. Use a poster, models, or diagrams to assist your report or presentation.

Can You Explain It?

Name: **Date:**

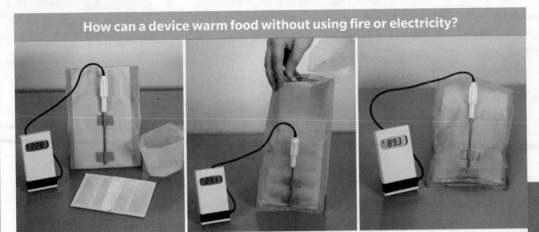

How can a device warm food without using fire or electricity?

Explore ONLINE!

 EVIDENCE NOTEBOOK

Refer to the notes in your Evidence Notebook to help you construct an explanation for how thermal energy could be released and transferred in order to warm food in a flameless cooking device.

1. State your claim. Make sure your claim fully explains how a device can warm food without using fire or electricity.

2. Summarize the evidence you have gathered to support your claim and explain your reasoning.

Checkpoints

Answer the following questions to check your understanding of the lesson.
Use the table to answer Question 3.

3. When ammonium chloride is mixed into water to form a solution, the solution absorbs thermal energy. Which process might represent 3 g of ammonium chloride mixed into a certain amount of water, and which process might represent 6 g mixed into the same amount of water?

Process	Temperature change (°C)
E	3.0
F	5.0
G	−4.0
H	−7.0

   A. Process E represents 3 g and Process F represents 6 g.

   B. Process F represents 3 g and Process E represents 6 g.

   C. Process G represents 3 g and Process H represents 6 g.

   D. Process H represents 3 g and Process G represents 6 g.

4. A high-quality sleeping bag will keep you warm even during a winter camping trip high in the mountains. How do you stay warm when the air around you is very cold?

   A. The sleeping bag produces thermal energy that keeps you warm.

   B. The sleeping bag transfers thermal energy from the air to your body.

   C. The sleeping bag slows the transfer of thermal energy produced by your body into the air.

   D. The sleeping bag increases the production of thermal energy by your body.

5. Samples of baking soda and vinegar at room temperature are mixed together. The resulting solution has a lower temperature than the original temperature of the vinegar. Which statement correctly describes how the system could be modified so that thermal energy is absorbed faster?

   A. Decrease the amount of baking soda used.

   B. Increase the concentrations of the chemicals used.

   C. Increase the size of the container used.

   D. Decrease the temperature of the environment so more energy flows away from the solution.

Use the photos to answer Question 6.

6. Which statement correctly describes what is occurring in the photos? Choose all that apply.

   A. The hand warmer is absorbing thermal energy.

   B. The hand warmer is releasing thermal energy.

   C. The hand warmer's temperature increased.

   D. The liquid in the hand warmer underwent a chemical process.

Interactive Review

Complete this page to review the main concepts of the lesson.

Systems can be used to model the flow of energy between objects.

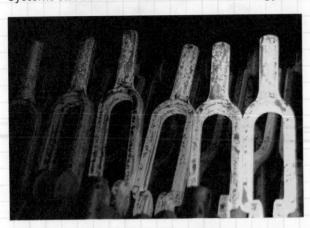

A. Why is it useful to model systems that use energy?

Chemical processes can release or absorb thermal energy.

B. Explain how different factors affect how thermal energy is absorbed or released by a chemical process.

A chemical process can be used in a device designed to release or absorb thermal energy.

C. Describe the process that you would go through when deciding on a chemical reaction to use in a device.

Choose one of the activities to explore how this unit connects to other topics.

Health Connection

The Chemistry of Digestion When you eat food, it is physically changed into small pieces through chewing. Carbohydrates, proteins, and fats are then chemically changed by reactions with enzymes and are absorbed into the bloodstream. Carbohydrates are converted to glucose, proteins become amino acids, and fats become glycerol and fatty acids.

Research the main category of your favorite food: carbohydrates, proteins, or fats. Then investigate how long it takes for that food to be chemically converted in your body and how your body uses the digested products. Create a short presentation on your findings.

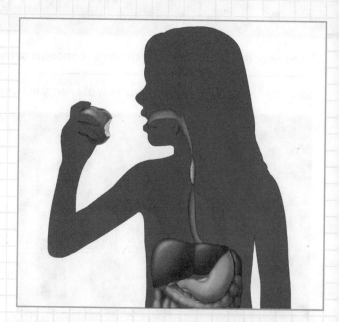

Environmental Science Connection

Acid Rain Burning fossil fuels produces sulfur dioxide and nitrogen oxides. These oxides react with water and oxygen in the atmosphere, producing sulfuric acid and nitric acid. Acid rain results when these products are carried to the ground with precipitation. Acid rain is harmful when it gets into soil and waterways because it can damage structures and organisms.

Research a specific animal or plant, and describe how it is affected by chemical reactions from acid rain. Create a pamphlet, including visuals, to showcase your findings.

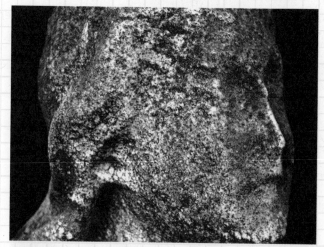

This statue has been damaged by acid rain.

Art Connection

Film Photography Reactions Silver chloride can be used for photography. When it is exposed to light, it reacts to darken the exposed parts of photographic paper. This process was used to create the images seen in some historic photographs.

Research the history of chemical photography and important individuals who contributed to the development of photographic processes. Create a timeline with descriptions of significant dates and example images.

This photo was processed using silver chloride development.

Name: _____   Date: _____

Complete this review to check your understanding of the unit.

Use the photos of eggs to answer Questions 1–3.

1. The image of the fried eggs is / is not an example of a chemical reaction. The image of the whisked eggs is / is not an example of a chemical reaction.

2. Which of the following statements are true about the reaction rates of cooked eggs? Circle all that apply.

   A. Increasing the temperature causes the reaction to occur more slowly.

   B. Increasing the temperature causes the reaction to occur more quickly.

   C. Increasing the temperature causes the eggs' particles to have more energy and move faster.

   D. Increasing the temperature causes the eggs' particles to lose energy and move more slowly.

3. Other than frying an egg, what is another way an egg can undergo a chemical change?

   A. scrambling a raw egg in a bowl

   B. mixing two eggs together in a bowl

   C. boiling an egg in hot water

   D. dropping an egg on the floor

Use the graph of reaction time data to answer Question 4.

4. Why does increasing the temperature of the water increase the rate of the chemical reaction in the graph?

   A. Faster moving particles will come into contact with each other less frequently.

   B. Faster moving particles will come into contact with each other more frequently.

   C. Changing the temperature does not change the motion of the particles.

   D. Warmer water contains more water particles.

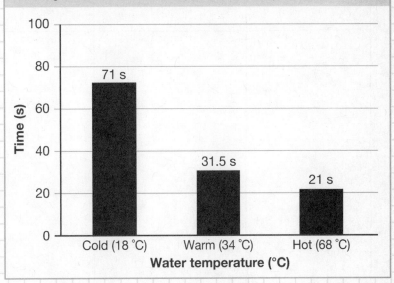

Effect of Temperature on Effervescent Tablets

This graph shows the time it takes for an effervescent tablet to finish reacting in water at different temperatures.

5. Complete the table by providing descriptions of how each of type of change relates to the properties of matter.

Properties of Matter	Physical Changes	Chemical Reactions	Changes in Energy
Arrangement of Atoms	During physical changes, the arrangment of atoms (molecular structure) of a substance remains the same.		
Physical Properties of Matter			
Chemical Properties of Matter			

Name: _____   Date: _____

Use the image of the grill and the molecular model to answer Questions 6–9.

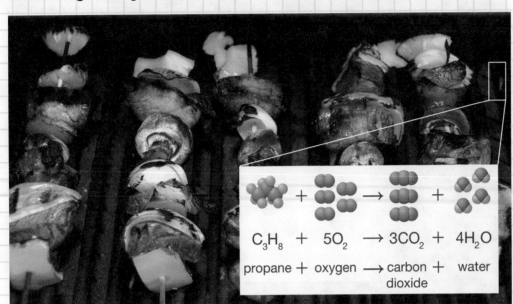

This food is cooking on a gas grill. The flames in the grill are a result of the reaction of propane gas with oxygen, as shown in the molecular model.

$$C_3H_8 + 5O_2 \rightarrow 3CO_2 + 4H_2O$$

propane + oxygen → carbon dioxide + water

6. Identify the reactants and products in the propane reaction, and list the number of each type of atom involved in the reaction.

7. What are some indicators that the food on the grill is undergoing a chemical reaction?

8. Describe the flow of thermal energy between the grill and the food, and what happens to particles in the food during this energy transfer.

9. What are some other ways that the reaction rate of the cooking food can be increased? Explain your answers.

Use the image of rusting bike and the molecular model to answer Questions 10–13.

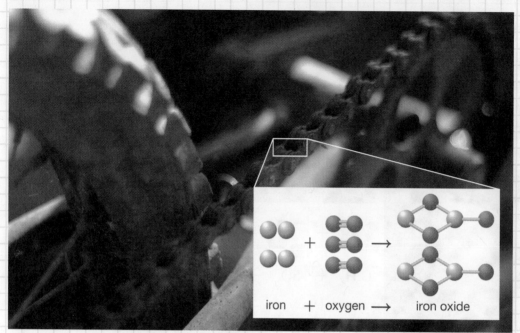

The rust forming on this bike is the product of a chemical reaction between iron and oxygen, as shown in the molecular model.

iron + oxygen ⟶ iron oxide

10. Describe how particles of iron (Fe) and oxygen (O_2) react to produce iron oxide (Fe_2O_3), also known as rust.

11. Write a balanced chemical equation based on the molecular model shown in the image. Describe the equation in a sentence.

12. The formation of iron oxide is a slow reaction that releases thermal energy. Describe what that means and explain the transfer of energy that is occurring.

13. Salt can act as a catalyst to the formation of iron oxide. What would happen if the bike was exposed to salt water?

Name: Date:

Save the Sea Turtle Eggs!

As a marine biologist, you are responsible for transporting sea turtle eggs that may be in danger after a storm. It is important to keep the eggs at a safe temperature (approximately 27 °C to 33 °C) for the 30 minutes it takes to drive to the animal hospital. You have three possible combinations of materials available to create an egg warmer to maintain the proper temperature:

- ammonium nitrate crystals and a pouch of water
- fine iron powder, salt, and water
- sodium acetate solution and a small metal disc

The steps below will help guide your research to develop an egg warmer.

Engineer It

1. **Define the Problem** Clearly define the criteria and constraints associated with the design of the egg warmer.

Engineer It

2. **Conduct Research** Research each of the three possible material combinations you could use to make an egg warmer. Are you looking for a chemical process that releases or absorbs thermal energy?

3. **Analyze Data** Create a decision matrix to analyze each material option. Describe the strengths and weaknesses of each choice.

4. **Identify and Recommend a Solution** Based on your research, construct a written explanation describing which combination of materials would make the best egg warmer. How would you design the warmer to safely carry eggs?

5. **Communicate** Prepare a presentation of your recommendation explaining the best materials and design to make a portable egg warmer.

✓ **Self-Check**

	I identified the problem.
	I researched the three combinations of materials to determine how well they meet the criteria and constraints of the problem.
	I analyzed my research and data to create a decision matrix.
	My solution is based on evidence from research, data, and an analysis of my decision matrix.
	My recommended design was clearly communicated to others.

The Chemistry of Materials

Paint pigments were originally made from natural substances derived from plants, animals, or minerals. Many paint pigments have now been replaced with human-made substances.

Synthetic, or human-made, materials surround us and are used in nearly every type of industry. Whether synthetics are made to be lighter, stronger, or less expensive than their naturally-sourced alternatives, these materials improve our lives in many ways. In this unit, you will investigate the relationship between natural resources and synthetic materials. You will also explore how synthetic materials are designed to have useful properties, and how the life cycles of synthetic materials impact society.

Why It Matters

Here are some questions to consider as you work through the unit. Can you answer any of the questions now? Revisit these questions at the end of the unit to apply what you discover.

Questions	Notes
Think about one of your favorite items that you use frequently. Do you think this item is made from natural (found in nature) or synthetic (human-made) materials?	
If an item is made from natural materials, what might happen if those materials are no longer available?	
How do items made from synthetic materials compare to items made from natural materials?	
Can an item made from synthetic materials be recycled?	
What might happen if the recycling programs currently in place for paper, plastic, and aluminum were discontinued?	

Unit Starter: Recognizing the Origins of Synthetic Materials

All synthetic materials are originally derived from natural materials. Examine each synthetic material below, and match it with the natural resource from which it is made.

1. Match each material made by humans on the right with the natural material used to make it on the left.

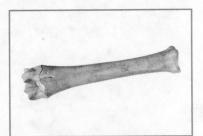

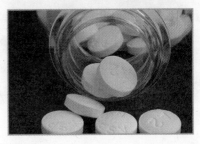

Go online to download the Unit Project Worksheet to help you plan your project.

Unit Project

Life Cycle of Synthetic Materials

Become a life cycle engineer! Choose a product made from synthetic materials, and research the life cycle for that material. Then, choose one stage of the product's life cycle to analyze, and propose an improvement to that process.

Natural and Synthetic Materials

The material that makes up these fabrics is ideal for clothing. Fabric can be made with natural or synthetic materials.

By the end of this lesson . . .

you will be able to explain how synthetic materials are designed and made to have properties that make them useful.

CAN YOU EXPLAIN IT?

How can a plastic kayak be made from oil?

crude oil

The synthetic material that makes up this kayak cannot be harvested or mined. It is made from crude oil, which is found naturally on Earth. Scientists and engineers have developed different types of plastics with different properties. Some synthetic materials make great kayaks, and others make beautiful fabrics.

1. How do the properties of the oil and of the plastic of the kayak differ? What makes the plastic a good choice for kayak material?

2. How do you think oil could be made into a plastic kayak?

EVIDENCE NOTEBOOK As you explore this lesson, consider how oil can be made into a plastic kayak.

Exploring Materials Science

The objects that surround you help shape your day. They might be simple, such as socks, or more complex, such as a tablet computer. The photo shows some objects you might use in your classroom. The materials that the objects are made of influence the way you use them. For example, a flag can bend in the wind. The fabric allows it to move freely. Fabric is useful for flags, but it would not make a good desk. A desk needs to be strong enough so that you can lean on it while you write.

3. Identify three classroom objects. What kinds of materials do you think make up these objects?

This classroom contains objects made of many different types of materials.

Materials

All of the objects around you are made of different kinds of materials. A material is a substance or mixture of substances that make up an object. There are many types of materials, from cotton in socks to plastic in part of the chair you are sitting in. Metals, plastics, glass, wood, and ceramics are all materials. Liquids, such as fuels or inks, are also materials. Most objects, from a pencil to a giant monster truck, are made of more than one material.

Many materials make up this monster truck. It has oil lubricating its moving parts, fuel, a metal body and engine parts, glass windows, fabric seats, and rubber tires.

Physical Properties

Every material has its own set of *physical properties*, which are properties that can be observed without changing the identity of the material. Glass has physical properties that are different from the physical properties of plastic or cotton. You can see through glass, and it breaks easily. You can see through the plastic of a water bottle, but it usually bends before it breaks. Cotton fabric is not see-through, and it changes shape easily. The transparency of a material and how easily it breaks or bends are physical properties. You can observe them without changing the material into a new material. The glass could be broken into many small pieces, but all of those small pieces are made of glass.

Some physical properties, such as mass and volume, depend on the amount of matter in a given sample. Others properties, such as whether something is hard or soft, do not depend on the amount of matter in a sample.

4. Think about the materials you interact with every day. How would you describe their physical properties? Add check marks to the table below to show whether each material has the properties listed.

Material	Hard	Bendable	Floats	Waterproof
cotton fabric		✓		
clear plastic of a water bottle				
steel				
wood				

You can observe some physical properties, such as color, shape, or state, by looking at a material. Other properties must be determined through tests or measurements. For example, you can measure the mass and volume of a material to determine its density. Density helps to determine whether a material will sink or float in water. Other measurable physical properties include boiling point, melting point, and hardness.

5. Engineer It Why is it important for engineers to determine the physical properties of materials? Use an example from the table to support your answer.

Chemical Properties

Materials can also be described by their *chemical properties*. Chemical properties describe a material's ability to undergo chemical reactions and form new substances. These properties are tested by attempting to change the identity of a substance.

Flammability, which is the ability to react with oxygen and burn, is a chemical property. Wood, paper, cotton fabric, and plastics are flammable. They can all burn. Steel and glass are not flammable. They do not burn.

Reactivity is another chemical property. Reactivity describes how a material reacts with another substance. The ability to react with oxygen is a type of reactivity. Iron reacts with oxygen to form rust. Rust is a new substance that has chemical and physical properties that are different from the properties of iron and oxygen.

Chemical Properties of Materials

Paper has the chemical property of flammability. You have to see the paper burning to observe this property. As the paper burns, the substances in the paper react with oxygen in the air and change into new substances.

Iron has the chemical property of reactivity with oxygen. Rust, a new substance, forms during the reaction. Rust has different chemical and physical properties than iron and oxygen have.

6. Why is it important to identify the chemical properties of materials? Select all answers that apply.

    A. Materials that have a low melting point would be dangerous to use when temperatures are hot.

    B. Flammable materials would be dangerous to use near a fire.

    C. A material's reactivity affects how long it will last under certain conditions.

    D. A material's ability to break or bend affects how well it will work for certain uses.

Chemical Makeup

Even though a given material has certain chemical and physical properties, most materials are not pure substances. A **pure substance** is matter that is composed of only one type of basic particle. Elements, such as iron, and compounds, such as the cellulose in wood, are pure substances. The *chemical makeup* of a material refers to the types and amounts of the pure substances in the material. For example, the cast iron that is used to make cookware and automobile parts is not pure iron. Small amounts of carbon, silicon, and other elements are mixed into the iron.

Materials for Different Uses

The chemical makeup of a material affects its chemical and physical properties. Together, chemical and physical properties determine how a material can be used. Consider the properties of glass and cast iron, which have different chemical makeups. The main criteria for a window are that it lets in light and has low reactivity so that it does not become cloudy. Because of its chemical makeup, glass is transparent and does not bend. It does not burn or react easily with oxygen. These properties of glass make it useful for windows. However, glass is not a good material for a car engine because it breaks easily. But cast iron is strong and hard, melts at a very high temperature, and is not flammable. So, cast iron is much more useful when making some car engine parts. Glass, iron, and other materials are used in different ways when building cars. These different materials meet the needs of the application.

7. Think about the properties of each material in the table below. Add a check mark to show whether each material would be good for each use.

Material	Building construction	Rain protection	Boats	Bed sheets
cotton fabric				✓
clear plastic of a water bottle				
steel				
wood				

Relate the Properties and Uses of Materials

8. The chemical and physical properties of a material affect how it is used. Look at the materials listed in the table below. Think about how you have seen each of these materials used. How do its properties meet the needs of those uses? Have you observed its chemical properties? For each material, list at least two physical properties, one chemical property, and three uses.

Material	Properties	Uses
aluminum	waterproof can be shaped bendable does not react in air	foil to cover food bike parts cans
hard plastic		
concrete		

Analyzing Natural Resources

If you go on a picnic in the park, you are surrounded by nature. Trees, grass, birds, rocks, and water are all a part of nature. The fruit in your picnic basket comes from nature. In fact, many of the materials around you every day come from nature, even the materials found inside your classroom. A desk is made by people, but the wood of the desk comes from trees. The metal comes from rocks. The fabric of your cotton clothing is made from cotton plants. Even chalk originally came from nature.

The materials and objects at this picnic are obtained from different sources.

9. What materials do you see in the photo? Which of those materials come from nature?

Natural Resources

Trees are a natural resource. A **natural resource** is a substance, material, object, or source of energy that is found in nature and is useful or valuable to humans. Humans use natural resources as sources of food and fuel. They may also use them to make other substances or materials. Some resources are used in many ways. Trees are used to produce lumber and paper, and wood from trees is sometimes used as fuel for heating people's homes.

Natural resources may be living things or nonliving things. Plants and animals provide food and materials, such as cotton, wool, and leather. Rocks and ores provide building materials, such as granite and iron. Sources of energy, such as coal, petroleum, natural gas, and sunlight, are also natural resources.

10. Choose an object near you. Explain whether the materials that make up the object are natural resources.

Material and Energy Resources

Animals and plants provide food, materials, and fuel. Cows give us meat, milk, and materials for leather. Corn gives us food and materials to make fuel and starch.

Metals come from ores that are mined. Copper is separated from other materials in this ore by chemical reactions and physical processes.

11. Describe how you use two living and two nonliving natural resources every day.

Properties

Natural resources have physical and chemical properties that make them useful. Some natural resources are used primarily for their physical properties. Copper is a good conductor of electricity and is used to make wire. Granite, a type of rock, is hard and dense. It is used in buildings. Natural resources are even used for their color. Many dyes were once made from plants. For example, indigo, a blue dye that gives jeans their color, is made from the indigo plant.

Some natural resources are mainly used for their chemical properties. Fuels such as petroleum, coal, and natural gas are highly flammable. They are used as fuels. Other resources, such as metals, are not flammable. They can be used to build stoves and cookware.

Plant materials, such as the grains stored in these silos, are made of many different substances, including cellulose. Cellulose makes plants useful in the manufacturing of paper, fabric, and building materials.

Chemical Makeup

Natural resources have many different chemical makeups. Most of the elements in the periodic table occur naturally—from aluminum to gold to uranium. However, very few elements are found in their pure form. Instead, they are combined in different ways in the compounds found in nature. Graphite is a form of pure carbon found in nature. Carbon also combines with other elements, such as oxygen and hydrogen, to make the huge variety of substances in living things.

Most natural resources are mixtures of substances. Rocks are mixtures of different compounds. Petroleum is a mixture of carbon-based compounds. Plants and animals are made up of many substances. Cellulose is one of the many substances found in plants. It is the main substance in cotton fabric and it makes wood strong.

Graphite is found naturally. It is soft and feels greasy. It is used to make pencil lead and lubricants.

Natural Resources for Different Uses

The way people use natural resources has changed as technologies and needs have changed. Ancient civilizations made tools from copper because pure copper was found in nature. They eventually learned to mix copper with other metals to make bronze. Today, copper is used to make electrical wire and is found in computer parts.

The resources used to meet needs have also changed. People have used trees for building materials and energy for a long time. However, once engines were invented, the use of electricity spread and the use of fossil fuels for energy increased. Wood is still used in building materials, but the use of steel has made taller buildings possible.

A hickory tree is made up of many substances that give it certain physical and chemical properties.

Hickory wood is flammable. When it burns, energy is released.

Hickory wood is strong and hard. It is used for floors because it does not dent or scratch easily.

12. Write some of the chemical and physical properties and uses of each natural resource shown in the photos below.

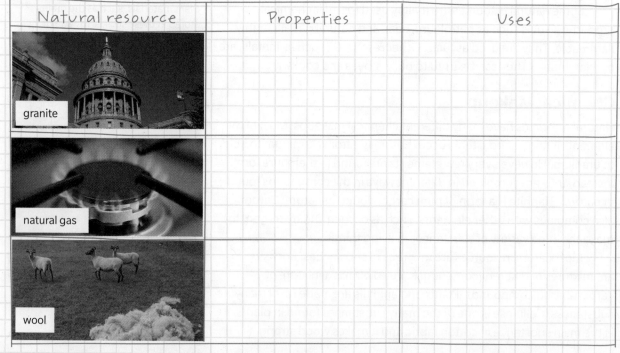

Natural resource	Properties	Uses
granite		
natural gas		
wool		

Do the Math
Analyze Natural Resource Use

A single natural resource may be used in different ways. Trees are used as building materials, to make paper, for fuel, and for other applications. The way wood is used depends on the type of wood, the size of the tree, and the quality of the wood. Saw mills inspect the properties of the logs before deciding how to process them. On average, saw mills use about 25% of the wood for lumber and other building materials, 25% for paper, 35% for fuel, and 15% for other uses. The percentages may vary from mill to mill depending on the logs that they accept and the way they process the wood.

After being cut down, trees are sent to mills where they are cut and processed into lumber products.

13. A saw mill produces about 28 m³ of dried lumber each day. About 70% of the lumber is cut into boards for use in construction, 25% is used to make thin sheets of wood used in plywood, and 5% is ground into pulp and used for paper products. Fill in the table below with the cubic meters of wood that are turned into each type of material each day.

Lumber produced	70% boards	25% plywood	5% paper
28 m³			

14. It takes about 38 m³ of boards and plywood to build an average-size, single-family home. Can an average-size, single-family home be built with one day's output from the saw mill? About how many days will it take for the saw mill to produce enough lumber to build a neighborhood of 100 average-size homes?

Getty Images

Investigating Synthetic Materials

The materials that make up many objects around you are not natural materials. If you look around the room, you will see a lot of plastic—in chairs, the parts of pens, eyeglasses, shoes, and even some fabrics. You will not find plastic occurring naturally in the environment. Plastic must be made using chemical processes.

Many materials that are not plastic are also not natural materials. The bicycle frame in the photo might look like painted metal, but it is much stronger and lighter than metal. Plastic and carbon fibers are mixed together to make a new material. In this case, the new material is made by a physical process and has properties of both plastic and carbon fibers.

A bicycle is made of many kinds of materials. Some are natural materials and others are made by chemical or physical process that form a new material.

15. **Discuss** On a separate sheet of paper, make a list of the parts of the bicycle in the photo and the materials that they might be made of. Sort your list into materials that might be natural resources and ones that might not be natural resources. With a partner, compare and discuss your lists. Revise your list as you come to an agreement about the types of materials used in the bike. Share your final list with the class.

Synthetic Materials

Most parts of a bicycle are synthetic materials rather than natural materials. **Synthetic materials** are human-made materials that are produced using natural or synthetic materials. Plastics are one type of synthetic material. There are many types of plastic, from the soft plastic that makes up a water bottle to the harder plastic that is used to make eyeglass lenses. Glass and ceramics are also synthetic materials. You will not find clear window glass in nature. Many foods, medicines, and personal care products are synthetic materials or contain synthetic materials. Some fuels, such as biodiesel and ethanol, are synthetic materials as well.

16. Which of the following items are most likely made from synthetic materials: a drinking glass, orange juice, a dinner plate, a paper bag, an insulated lunch bag? Explain your reasoning.

Synthetic materials, such as this nylon, can be made in a lab.

Formation

Most synthetic materials are formed through chemical reactions. The starting substances, called *reactants*, may be natural or synthetic substances. The diagram shows the reaction that forms polyethylene, a solid used to make plastic bottles. The starting substance is ethylene, a gas made from crude oil. The ethylene molecules join together to form polyethylene, the product. Starting reactants change into new substances in all chemical reactions. Bonds between the atoms break and new bonds form. As a result, the atoms are rearranged to make one or more new substances.

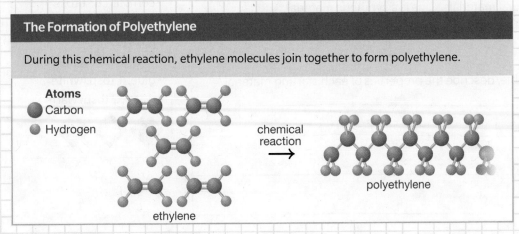

The Formation of Polyethylene

During this chemical reaction, ethylene molecules join together to form polyethylene.

Atoms
● Carbon
● Hydrogen

chemical reaction

polyethylene

ethylene

17. Act With a group, model how ethylene molecules react to form polyethylene.

Properties

The properties of a pure substance depend on the identity and the arrangement of the atoms that make up the substance. Therefore, the products of a reaction have different chemical and physical properties than the starting materials have. Ethylene and polyethylene have different properties because their atoms are arranged differently.

Some synthetic materials, such as composites, are made by mixing together materials to form a new material. Mixing is a physical change. The materials that make up the composite keep their original properties, but the composite material also has new properties. Concrete, plywood, and fiberglass are composites.

18. How do the properties of polyethylene compare to the properties of ethylene?

19. Why do synthetic materials have different properties than the materials used to make them?

EVIDENCE NOTEBOOK

20. How might the substances in oil change into the substances that make up the plastic of a kayak? Record your evidence.

Hands-On Lab
Make a Synthetic Material

You will use a chemical reaction to make a ball out of a synthetic material.
Your reactants are borax, cornstarch, water, and glue. Borax is mined from rocks. Cornstarch is separated out from corn kernels. Borax, water, and cornstarch are natural materials. Glue is a synthetic material.

Procedure

STEP 1 In the table, describe the properties of each starting material.

Materials	Properties
borax	
cornstarch	
water	
white glue	

STEP 2 Make a borax solution by adding $1\frac{1}{2}$ tsp borax to 2 tbsp warm water in a cup. Stir until the borax disappears.

STEP 3 Add 1 tbsp glue to the second cup. If you are using food coloring, add about 3 drops.

STEP 4 To the glue, add $\frac{1}{2}$ tsp of the borax solution and 1 tbsp of cornstarch.

STEP 5 Wait 10 seconds, and then stir the contents of the cup until you cannot stir anymore.

STEP 6 Roll the mixture in your hands until it forms a smooth ball. Explore the properties of the new material.

Analysis

STEP 7 How do the properties of the synthetic material you made compare to the properties of the starting materials?

STEP 8 What caused the properties to change?

How Synthetic Materials Are Used

Synthetic materials have a wide variety of chemical and physical properties. Some are very strong and hard, while others are soft and flexible. Some have low reactivity and others undergo very specific chemical reactions. The synthetic material used to make a bouncy ball is soft and bounces. The carbon fiber reinforced bike frame is strong and light. A medicine reacts in the body in a certain way. The properties of each of these synthetic materials make them well-suited for the ways that they are used.

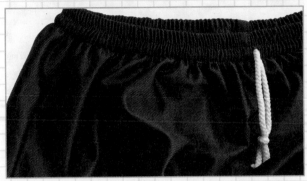

Polyester is a synthetic material that is used to make clothes. It is lightweight and does not shrink when washed and dried.

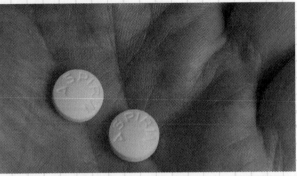

Aspirin, in pill form, is a synthetic material that is used as medicine. It reacts in the body to relieve pain.

21. Nylon is a synthetic material that can be made into string. Mountain climbers use ropes that are made of nylon string that is woven together and braided. What properties of the nylon rope are important for the mountain climbers who use it?

Relate the Properties and Uses of a Synthetic Material

Fiberglass is a composite material made of glass fibers mixed in plastic. The mixture of the glass fibers and plastic makes a strong, lightweight material that can be molded into many shapes. Fiberglass does not conduct electricity well.

22. Based on its properties, list two other ways in which fiberglass would be a useful material. Explain how the properties of fiberglass are important for each use.

Fiberglass is a composite synthetic material.

_____

_____

_____

_____

_____

Analyzing the Design of Synthetic Materials

Take a glance around the room and you will see many types of synthetic materials. Why are there so many kinds of synthetic materials? Scientists and engineers design them to meet specific needs. The polyester used in clothes needs to be able to be drawn into soft threads. The glass in a window needs to let in light. Engineers have even designed glass, such as the glass in the photo, that does not break as easily as other glass.

23. What are two uses of glass? How do the needs of each type of glass differ for these uses?

This glass might shatter when an object hits it, but it does not break apart. It can help reduce damage when it is used for windows in places where there are hurricanes.

Types of Synthetic Materials

All synthetic materials are made by chemical processes instead of being extracted from a natural resource. Plastic is one type of synthetic material. The starting materials for most plastics come from oil, which is a natural resource.

Plastics are polymers. **Polymers** are long molecules that are made up of five or more repeating units. Recall the reaction of ethylene to form polyethylene. Polyethylene is a polymer that is made of repeating ethylene units.

24. Nonstick cooking pans are easy to clean because they are coated with a polymer. What properties of the polymer meet the specific needs of this application?

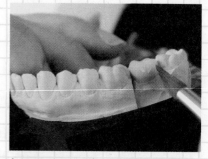
A strong composite made of a polymer and glass is used in tooth-colored fillings and crowns.

Composites are synthetic materials that are made from a mixture of two or more materials. Polymers are used to make some composites, such as fiberglass. Dental fillings and tooth-shaped caps that cover teeth, called crowns, can be made using composite material made from a polymer and glass. This material is strong and the same color as teeth.

EVIDENCE NOTEBOOK

25. How could a chemical reaction change oil into a new material with different properties? What properties of the plastic are important for a kayak? Record your evidence.

Medicine

Most medicines are synthetic materials that are designed to have specific chemical properties. Medicines are used to treat specific conditions, such as diabetes, pain, and allergies. People with diabetes take insulin. While some substances, such as insulin, are found naturally in the body or environment, it is often easier and more economical to synthesize the substance. Genetically modified bacteria produce most of the insulin that is used as medicine today.

Materials for Products

Synthetic materials are used in many products, including paints, building materials, clothing, and electronics. Different materials are made by using different combinations of starting substances, which may be natural or synthetic materials. Plastics can have a variety of properties for different uses—from thin plastic films used for sandwich bags to hard plastic used for car bumpers. Materials such as concrete and plywood are used in construction. Some synthetic materials even glow to light up computer screens.

Synthetic materials are designed for use in some electronic screens to provide properties such as resolution and brightness.

26. **Engineer It** Synthetic materials such as organic light-emitting diodes, called *OLEDs*, are used to make some computer and television screens. These materials glow when an electric current is applied to them. OLEDs that glow different colors are combined to make screens. What properties of a screen are important to you when you are using your computer or phone? What properties of OLED materials would engineers try to produce when they make the materials?

Foods

Synthetic materials are added to many foods today to help them last longer or add color, flavor, or sweetness. Preservatives, such as citric acid, make food last longer by slowing chemical reactions or the growth of mold and bacteria. Some synthetic materials in food are found in nature. Citric acid and banana flavoring are found in fruits or seeds. However, citric acid and banana flavoring are also made from other materials.

Fuels

Some fuels are synthetic materials that are made from natural materials. Ethanol is added to gasoline. Ethanol is made from materials in plants, such as corn and wood. Algae can also be used to make fuel. Algae produce oils that can be turned into biodiesel. The algae may also be genetically modified to produce more oil than they normally would.

Algae make oils that can be turned into biodiesel, which is a fuel that is used in some vehicles.

27. The plant and algae resources used to make biofuels can be regrown after they are used. How does this make biofuels different from fossil fuels?

Determine Sources and Uses of Synthetic Materials

Vanilla is a common flavor in many foods, including ice cream, cookies, and cereal. It is also used as a scent in candles. It is found naturally in vanilla beans, but most vanilla flavoring that is added to food is the synthetic substance vanillin. Synthetic vanillin is chemically the same as the main substance that gives vanilla beans their vanilla flavor and scent. How and why is synthetic vanillin made?

You can find information about how synthetic vanillin, or almost any synthetic material, is made and how it is used. However, some of that information may not be reliable. When you are looking for information about chemical reactions, scientific journals with research articles are a reliable source of information. But, they may not be easy to understand. University websites, chemical societies, and science magazines are good places to look. They try to present accurate information. Company websites may be reliable sources for certain types of information. The companies are experts on the way they make the material and the properties of the material. However, the companies also have biases because they make money from the material. Any websites for organizations that are trying to promote certain points of view are likely to present biased information.

Possible sources of information
a nationally accredited college research department
an independently funded science organization
a government website
a national research lab
a company that makes the material
an organization that supports a natural diet
a society of professional materials scientists or chemists
an organization that promotes the use of food additives
a popular science magazine

28. Which of the sources listed above would be the most reliable sources of information about synthetic vanillin? Would some sources be reliable for certain types of information, but not others?

_____

_____

_____

_____

_____

29. Research how synthetic vanillin is made. What are the sources of the starting materials? Are there advantages or disadvantages to using synthetic vanillin? Should people choose foods with natural vanilla over synthetic vanillin? On a sheet of paper, write a marketing pitch for synthetic vanillin for a consumer audience.

Continue Your Exploration

Name: _____ **Date:** _____

Check out the path below or go online to choose one of the other paths shown.

How Oil Is Used

- **Hands-On Labs** ✋
- **Biomimicry**
- **Propose Your Own Path**

Go online to choose one of these other paths.

Crude oil is oil that comes directly from Earth's crust. It is most notably used for fuels, such as gasoline and diesel. Crude oil is also used to make plastics. In fact, crude oil provides the starting materials that are used to produce many synthetic materials, including medicines and food additives. The liquids in crude oil are separated by their boiling points through a process called refining. The diagram shows some of the uses of the different natural materials that are collected. Some of the natural materials are used as fuels, while others may undergo chemical reactions to produce synthetic materials with a wide range of chemical and physical properties.

Products Made from Crude Oil

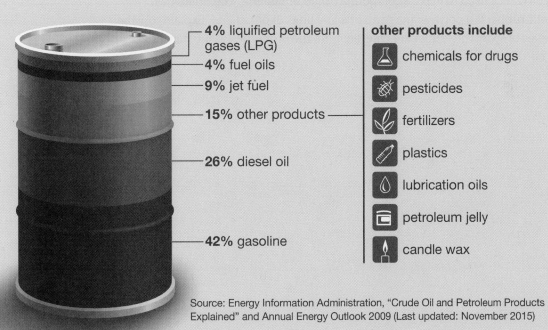

- **4%** liquified petroleum gases (LPG)
- **4%** fuel oils
- **9%** jet fuel
- **15%** other products
- **26%** diesel oil
- **42%** gasoline

other products include

- chemicals for drugs
- pesticides
- fertilizers
- plastics
- lubrication oils
- petroleum jelly
- candle wax

Source: Energy Information Administration, "Crude Oil and Petroleum Products Explained" and Annual Energy Outlook 2009 (Last updated: November 2015)

The majority of crude oil is used for fuels such as gasoline and diesel, but a small percentage of crude oil is used as starting material for synthetic materials and other products.

1. Based on the information in the text and the diagram of products made from crude oil, what natural and synthetic materials do you use that come from crude oil?

2. Look back at the image on the previous page. Think about all the products that are obtained from crude oil. How do the properties of the different fuels made with crude oil differ from the properties of the other materials made from crude oil?

3. Crude oil can be used to make a compound called butadiene, a colorless gas. Synthetic rubber is a polymer made up of many units of butadiene. Explain why the properties of synthetic rubber are different from the properties of substances in crude oil.

4. **Collaborate** In a group, make a list of products that are made of plastics or have plastic parts. Choose one product and do research to identify the type of polymer that makes up the plastic. Find out how it is made from materials in crude oil. Create a presentation to share with the class.

Can You Explain It?

Name: _____   Date: _____

How can a plastic kayak be made from oil?

crude oil

EVIDENCE NOTEBOOK

Refer to the notes in your Evidence Notebook to help you construct an explanation for how a plastic kayak can be made from crude oil.

1. State your claim. Make sure your claim fully explains how a plastic kayak can be made from oil.

2. Summarize the evidence you have gathered to support your claim, and explain your reasoning.

Checkpoints

Answer the following questions to check your understanding of the lesson.

Use the photo to answer Questions 3–4.

3. What properties are needed in the material used to make these items? Select all that apply.

    A. It breaks easily.

    B. It stretches.

    C. It is strong.

    D. It holds in air.

4. Some balloons are made of latex, which can be made from substances that come from crude oil. These substances undergo chemical reactions to form latex. The latex of the balloons is a *natural material / synthetic material.*

Use the photo to answer Questions 5–6.

5. The photo shows a field where some sports activities are performed. This solution can be achieved with natural or synthetic materials. Why might a synthetic material be the best choice for the solution?

    A. Synthetic materials can be designed to fit a certain need.

    B. Synthetic materials are easier to make than obtaining natural materials.

    C. The use of natural materials has a negative impact on the environment.

6. What properties of plastic make it useful for fake grass? Select all that apply.

    A. It can be colored green.

    B. It is durable.

    C. It can be made into thin strips.

    D. It breaks down in the sun.

---

7. Ceramic pots are made by heating clay to form a new material. Which statements describe how ceramics are made? Select all that apply.

    A. Ceramics are made by a physical change.

    B. Ceramics are made by a chemical reaction.

    C. The atoms in the starting materials rearrange when clay is heated.

    D. The ceramics have the same properties as the starting material.

8. How do the properties of a substance that is the result of a chemical reaction compare to the properties of the starting materials?

    A. The properties will stay the same.

    B. The properties will be different.

    C. The properties will stay the same and new properties will be added.

Interactive Review

Complete this section to review the main concepts of the lesson.

The ways materials are used depend on their physical and chemical properties.

A. How do the physical properties of materials help determine the ways in which they are used?

Natural resources are found in nature and are used by humans.

B. What properties of a natural resource make it useful to humans as a material or energy source?

Synthetic materials are made by people using chemical reactions or by mixing together materials.

C. Explain why chemical reactions are used to form synthetic materials.

Engineers design synthetic materials to meet specific needs.

D. Why are synthetic materials sometimes used when designing a way to improve existing materials?

The Life Cycle of Synthetic Materials

Artificial limbs are designed to meet specific needs. The materials in this prosthetic leg are both strong and flexible.

By the end of this lesson . . .

you will be able to describe how our use of synthetic materials impacts society.

CAN YOU EXPLAIN IT?

How can the same molecules that make up the bottles later be used to make the jacket?

Plastic bottles and polyester jackets are made of the same synthetic material.

1. Where have you seen plastic beverage bottles and polyester jackets?

2. Where do these bottles and jackets come from?

EVIDENCE NOTEBOOK As you explore this lesson, gather evidence to explain how the material in plastic bottles can be turned into a jacket.

Analyzing the Life Cycle of Synthetic Materials

You can find synthetic materials in your backpack, your closet, the refrigerator, and the medicine cabinet. Synthetic materials are materials that are made by humans using chemical processes. Synthetic materials are usually designed to have specific properties needed for a particular purpose. However, sometimes new materials are discovered by accident. For example, in the 1960s, Stephanie Kwolek was developing new polymers that could be used to make tires more durable. She discovered a new type of fiber that was extremely strong and lightweight. That fiber is Kevlar®. Its properties make it ideal for use in bulletproof vests and helmets.

3. How do the properties of Kevlar® determine how it is used?

Between the layers of black fabric in this bulletproof vest is a layer of protective synthetic material called Kevlar.

Synthetic Materials and Society

Engineers have designed different types of Kevlar® that have many uses. Some of the things Kevlar® is used in include vehicle armor, motorcycle racing gear, and tires.

Engineers also look for ways to improve existing materials or design new materials as the needs of society change. New materials have made cars more lightweight, which means they burn less gasoline. New medicines are developed as scientists learn more about the causes of diseases. New materials help computers work faster.

4. Which of the following might drive the development of new materials? Select all that apply.

A. a desire for affordable, fashionable clothing

B. an idea that air pollution should be reduced

C. a need for safe apartment buildings

D. a change in the availability of natural resources

Needs

Synthetic materials are developed to meet the needs of people. Some needs are basic, such as food and water, energy, housing, and transportation. But even these needs have changed. Foods are now shipped all over the world and may be stored for long periods of time before they reach consumers. Synthetic materials that preserve food help it last longer. The population has increased and cities have grown. Synthetic building materials have made it possible to build larger buildings to house more people and businesses.

Desires

What things would you like to buy—trendy clothes, shoes of a famous basketball player, video games, or a bike like your friends have? People's desires also affect the types of materials that are developed and the way they are used. Materials may be developed to make products people want, such as running shoes or bicycle frames. Synthetic materials may also make products more affordable.

Values

Values affect the development and use of materials. Your values include what you think is good and important. For example, some people think that all natural food is good for your health. They are likely to choose food without synthetic dyes and preservatives. These choices affect the food that companies make. Food scientists are likely to find natural materials to replace synthetic materials to meet consumer demand.

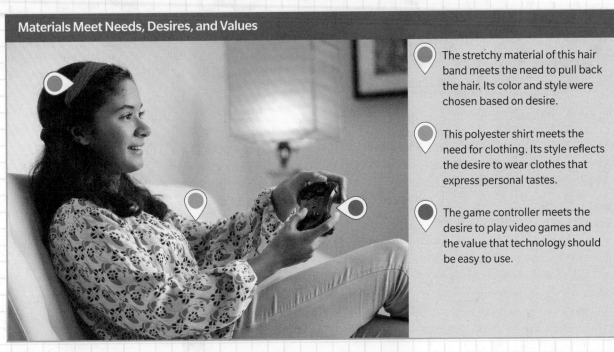

Materials Meet Needs, Desires, and Values

The stretchy material of this hair band meets the need to pull back the hair. Its color and style were chosen based on desire.

This polyester shirt meets the need for clothing. Its style reflects the desire to wear clothes that express personal tastes.

The game controller meets the desire to play video games and the value that technology should be easy to use.

5. In what ways are needs today different than they were 50 years ago?

6. Discuss Think about the plastic casing on a cell phone. Why do you think it is made of plastic? What needs, desires, or values were likely involved in its development?

Phases of the Life Cycle

The polyester in a shirt and the plastic in a cell phone case go through many steps before they reach you. The steps that a material or product goes through are called the *life cycle* of the material. One model of a life cycle includes five steps: obtaining natural resources, production, distribution, consumer use, and disposal. The life cycle describes where a product comes from, how it is used, and where it goes after it is used.

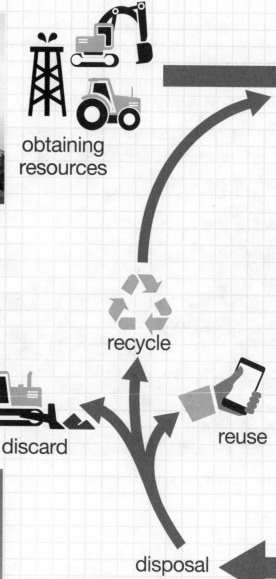

obtaining
resources

recycle

discard

reuse

disposal

Obtaining Resources

The first step in a life cycle is to obtain the resources needed to make the materials. These resources may be natural resources or recycled materials. A cell phone contains many materials, including metals, plastics, and glass. The metals are produced from ores that are mined. The starting material for plastic comes from crude oil, which is extracted from the ground. Glass is made from resources such as sand and limestone.

Disposal

Consumers dispose of products when they are done using them. At this point in the life cycle, products and the materials that they contain are discarded, recycled, or reused. Products may be discarded and end up in a landfill where they remain. Some products may be flushed down the drain, where they enter the wastewater system. Many products, including plastic containers and cell phones, may be recycled to produce new materials. Other products, such as electronic devices, may be refurbished and used again.

Production

During the production stage of a synthetic material, chemical reactions or mixing processes produce the materials in the product. The materials are then shaped into the various parts of the product. Then the parts are put together to make the finished product. Cell phones may be thin, but they have many tiny parts inside the plastic covering.

production

distribution

Distribution

Products must reach consumers, but they are rarely shipped directly from the factory to the consumer. They are likely to be shipped from where they are produced to a warehouse where they are stored. From there, products may be shipped to a store or directly to the consumer.

consumer use

Consumer Use

Consumers use products in different ways. Some products, such as food and medicine, are consumed. Other products, such as a paper plate, may only be used once. Products such as cell phones may be used frequently for a long time. Products may also be shared and reused by multiple consumers.

7. Follow the arrows and label the photos to show the life cycle of a nylon rope.

WORD BANK
- consumer use
- disposal
- distribution
- ~~obtaining resources~~
- production

obtaining resources

8. How else could the nylon rope be disposed of?

Relate Natural Resource Use and the Life Cycle

Natural resources are obtained during the first stage in the life cycle of a material or a product. However, all stages of the life cycle affect the use of natural resources. Some resources are used to make products. Other resources are used as energy resources. Consumers can reuse or recycle products to reduce the need to obtain more natural resources.

The availability of materials also affects how they are used. Some natural resources are scarce. Alternative materials that do not use those resources may be developed.

Excavators are used to harvest trees on a peatland forest in Indonesia's Borneo Island. Synthetic materials that come from trees include rayon fabric, plywood, and some rosin-based adhesives.

9. How can recycling rubber tires into materials that make playground and track surfaces affect the use of natural resources?

EVIDENCE NOTEBOOK

10. How can the end of the life cycle of a plastic bottle be the beginning of the life cycle of a polyester jacket? Record your evidence.

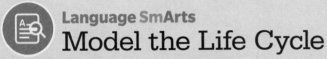

Language SmArts
Model the Life Cycle

11. Write a story about the life cycle of a plastic or paper shopping bag. Remember that plastic is made from petroleum and paper is made from trees.

_____

_____

_____

_____

_____

_____

_____

_____

_____

12. Draw In the space below, draw a diagram to model the life cycle of the plastic or paper bag.

Analyzing the Impact of Synthetic Materials

Diamonds can be a symbol of marriage or wealth for many people in the United States. In addition to being desired for their beauty, the hardness of diamonds makes them useful for industrial tasks such as cutting, grinding, drilling, and polishing. Diamonds are formed naturally deep within Earth, so they must be mined. An increase in the demand for diamonds means that more land must be mined.

Engineers can also make synthetic diamonds to help meet the need for diamonds. Synthetic diamonds usually cost less than natural diamonds. Also, they do not need to be mined.

13. How might the life cycle of synthetic diamonds affect society?

This thin sheet of Chemical Vapor Deposition (CVD) diamond is being held above other synthetic diamond stones. CVD diamonds can take six months to grow using methane gas and are one of the best conductors of heat in the world.

Impacts Throughout the Life Cycle

The impacts of a product containing synthetic materials can be determined by analyzing the product's life cycle. Each stage of the life cycle may have positive or negative effects on society and the environment. For example, producing cell phones provides people with jobs, but exposure to some materials used in the product may cause health problems if proper safety procedures are not used. Decisions at each stage of the life cycle can help decrease potential negative effects.

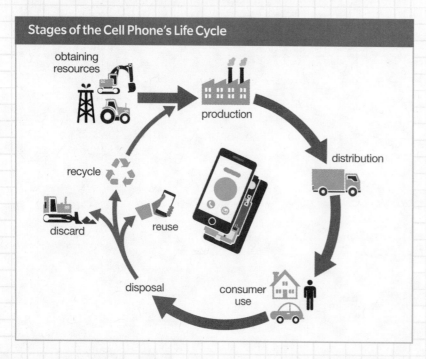

Stages of the Cell Phone's Life Cycle

obtaining resources — production — distribution — consumer use — disposal — discard — reuse — recycle

14. How might drilling for oil to make plastic used in a cell phone case impact society? Select all that apply.

A. Jobs are created for people who work for oil companies.

B. Oil spills at drilling sites can harm the environment.

C. Jobs are lost for people who produce alternative fuels.

D. Pollution from oil is reduced.

Obtaining Resources

Obtaining natural resources can have an impact on the environment. As resources are harvested, the tools used and the waste created can impact the environment. For example, mining and oil drilling can pollute Earth systems. And habitats are destroyed to make way for mines or oil rigs.

Obtaining natural resources can also affect the availability of a resource in the future. If we use a resource at a rate that is faster than it can be replenished, that resource will be nonrenewable. For example, the rate at which we have been using oil has depleted the supply faster than it can be replenished.

Society is also affected in other ways as we obtain natural resources. For example, mining and oil drilling create jobs and provide needed resources, but these jobs can be dangerous for workers.

On July 18, 2010, an explosion at the Deepwater Horizon oil drilling platform released an estimated 130 million gallons of oil into the Gulf of Mexico. Oil spills like this can damage the surrounding environment and all living things that depend on it.

Production

People are employed to produce synthetic materials and then make products out of them. These jobs are often located far away from where the materials are used. For example, most cell phones are manufactured outside of the United States. Factory jobs may provide workers with new opportunities. However, factory workers in other countries may not always have the same protections as workers in the United States have. They may work very long hours for low pay or work in unsafe conditions.

Production can also produce pollution and use energy. The chemical reactions that produce synthetic materials may also produce substances that are toxic. These toxins can pollute the air, water, and ground if they are not disposed of properly. Another source of air pollution during production can be the source of energy for the factories, such as coal power plants. Burning coal releases carbon dioxide that contributes to air pollution.

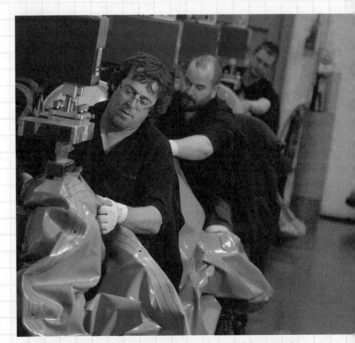

Workers in a plastics factory are making industrial strength plastic bags for use in construction.

Getty Images; (b) ©67photo/Alamy

Distribution

Today, synthetic materials and the products made from them are shipped around the world. Distribution systems are efficient and can move products to consumers quickly. Products are shipped on trucks, ships, and trains from factories to warehouses. They can also be transported to stores or directly to customers. As a result of these factors, materials and products are less expensive for consumers. However, the distribution stage also has a negative impact. It produces greenhouse gases and other pollutants as products are transported.

Global distribution allows cell phones to be made more affordably in other countries and shipped to stores in the United States.

Consumer Use

Using synthetic materials has both positive and negative effects. Many synthetic materials improve people's quality of life. For example, synthetic medicines can make people feel better and cure diseases. Cell phones help people stay connected over great distances.

Consumer use of synthetic materials can also have negative effects, which are sometimes caused by the choices consumers make. For example, people may use too much fertilizer. Excess fertilizer makes its way to streams, rivers, and oceans where it causes harmful blooms of algae.

Many products use energy and cause pollution when they are used. For example, cell phones need to be plugged in to be recharged and refrigerators constantly use energy.

Digital tablets can have a positive impact because they allow people who are far apart to communicate easily.

Disposal

When people increase their use of materials, the amount of material that is discarded also increases. A huge amount of waste goes to landfills every day. Landfills can be smelly, which is unpleasant for people who live nearby. Improper disposal of some materials can pollute the land and water in areas near and far away from landfills. As the waste breaks down, it produces gases such as methane and carbon dioxide. The methane may be collected and burned. Some landfills are even using methane as an energy resource.

Some waste does not reach landfills, such as when people throw trash along roads or natural areas. Plastic pollution harms animals. Sometimes they mistake it for food. When animals eat the plastic, they can die because it stays in their stomachs. Plastic can also become attached around parts of animals and cause harm to their bodies.

Reusing and recycling can reduce the materials sent to landfills. Materials are reused when they are used more than once. Consumers can also donate or share items so that someone else can use them. Recycling turns used materials into new materials that may be used again. Recycling saves energy and natural resources. It creates jobs for people who work in recycling businesses. For example, cell phone parts, such as metal and some plastics, can be recycled to make new materials. Plastic bottles can be recycled and spun into threads to make fabric.

A cell phone recycling technician works on old cell phones to recover metals and other materials that can be used again.

An employee at a cell phone company refurbishes a used cell phone that still works. The cell phone can then be resold and someone else can use it.

15. Why is it important for engineers to consider how a synthetic material will be disposed of when they are developing a new material?

Economic Impact of the Life Cycle

A material's life cycle impacts the economy in numerous ways. All stages of a life cycle provide people with jobs. People may also work in industries that support the life cycle, such as making equipment used for mining or repairing delivery trucks. The life cycle of materials can have a big impact on the economy of countries. Some countries depend on their natural resources, such as oil. Other countries depend on the production of materials and products. Changes to the costs of natural resources or the demand for materials affects the economy. For example, low oil prices can negatively affect the economy of a country that depends on oil extraction.

Do the Math | Analyze the Economics of Recycling

Recycling helps the environment by saving energy and reducing the use of natural resources. Because materials do not need to be extracted and made from scratch, recycled materials are often less expensive to produce. The cost of natural resources, the availability of recycled materials, and the processes used to make new materials all determine whether recycling materials is economically useful.

Plastic water bottles can be recycled to make plastic for new products.

16. A company needs to make at least 75,000 bottles. Twenty-one 20-oz. bottles can be made from one pound of plastic. New plastic costs 83 cents/pound. Recycled plastic costs 55 cents/pound. Determine the economic impact of using new materials and recycled materials.

    The company needs _____ pounds of plastic. The plastic needed to make all of the water bottles will cost the company _____ for new plastic and _____ for recycled plastic.

17. Compare the price of the materials needed to make 75,000 bottles. Which type of plastic is the less expensive choice? How much can the company save using the less expensive plastic?

Analyze Impact on Society

18. A new prescription drug has been approved to treat a certain disease. The substances used to make the drug come from pine trees. Choose two stages of the life cycle of the drug. Describe what impact on society the new drug might have in these two stages.

_____

_____

_____

_____

_____

_____

Relating Engineering and the Life Cycle

Engineers have shaped the life cycle of synthetic materials and the products made from them. You might realize that engineers are involved in producing cell phones. They are also involved in making simple products, such as disposable gloves and plastic bottles.

19. How can improvements that engineers make during a material's life cycle affect its impact on society and the environment?

Engineers designed this machine to test disposable gloves made from a polymer to make sure they do not leak.

The Role of Engineering in the Life Cycle

Cell phones have changed drastically since they were first invented. The first cell phones were large and could be used only to talk. Cell phones today are thin, sleek, and can be used to talk and text. They can also do almost anything a computer can do. These changes are the result of improvements that engineers made at some stages of a cell phone's life cycle. To improve cell phones, engineers define the criteria and constraints of a problem. These include the costs, safety, energy usage, potential pollution, and how the material needs to work. They find solutions by analyzing and testing possible solutions.

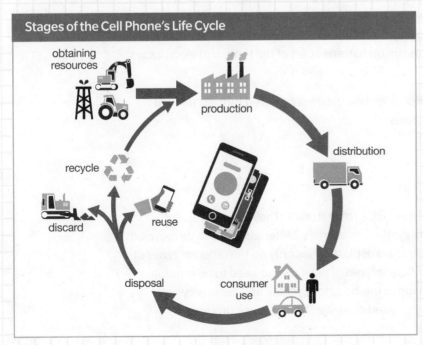

Stages of the Cell Phone's Life Cycle

obtaining resources
production
distribution
recycle
reuse
discard
disposal
consumer use

20. Discuss What roles might engineers play in the life cycle of a material? Discuss how they might be involved in extracting materials, making and improving materials and products, improving distribution, and sorting recyclables.

Obtaining Resources

Engineers develop and improve ways of finding and extracting natural resources. They design tools that are used to drill for oil. They have developed new ways of extracting natural gas. This provides access to resources that could not be extracted in the past.

21. What are two ways engineers might improve the way natural resources are obtained to reduce the impact on the environment?

This machine turns melted plastic into many plastic pieces that are all the same shape.

Production

Engineers play many roles in the production of synthetic materials. They oversee the production process. Engineers look for ways to make processes more efficient and cheaper. They figure out ways to minimize waste materials. Engineers also design and improve machines, like the one in the photo.

Distribution

Engineers solve problems to help make the processes involved with distribution more efficient. For example, engineers have helped improve product packaging so that it has less impact on the environment. Polystyrene foam packing peanuts were once widely used to cushion objects during shipping. The peanuts can be reused, but they cannot be easily recycled. Engineers have developed air-filled plastic pouches and packaging peanuts made out of cornstarch to replace the foam peanuts.

Consumer Use

Engineers design products to meet the needs and values of consumers. For example, they recognized consumers' concern about carbon dioxide emission from gas-powered cars. They worked with scientists to design cars that use less fuel and produce fewer pollutants. As a result, new hybrid cars run on batteries part of the time, and electric cars only use batteries.

22. What are some of the benefits of engineering vehicles powered by fuels derived from living organisms, called biofuels?

Disposal

Engineers play an important role in the recycling of materials. They have developed processes to recycle many natural and synthetic materials. Materials that can be recycled include metals, glass, paper, and many types of plastic. Not only do the different types of materials need to be separated, the different types of plastics also need to be separated from each other. Engineers have developed methods to separate and clean recycled materials. The materials can then be shredded or melted to make new products.

Hands-On Lab
Sort Synthetic Materials Using Properties

You will design a process to separate materials.

You can only use the physical properties of the materials, such as density and attraction to a magnet. Imagine your materials will be going directly from one step to another step. You cannot sort them by picking out the parts by hand. You may make screens with holes in them using scissors and cardboard.

MATERIALS
- bowl of water
- cardboard
- fan
- fine mesh sieve
- magnet
- materials to sort: marbles, metal paper clips, small balls of aluminum foil, plastic straws, pieces of paper
- scissors

Sorting Machine at Recycling Plant

People do sort some materials in recycling centers, but machines do a large part of the sorting based on the properties of the materials.

Procedure

STEP 1 Identify the criteria and constraints of the sorting process. Record your notes.

STEP 2 Discuss the properties of the materials and how you might use them to sort the materials. Record your conclusions.

STEP 3 Design a process to sort the materials. Describe your process.

STEP 4 Use the materials to make a model to test your sorting process. Record your results.

STEP 5 Revise your sorting process as needed to solve any problems you encountered during your tests. Record the changes you make to your process. Record the results of tests using your modified sorting process.

Analysis

STEP 6 What properties did you use to sort your materials?

STEP 7 Prepare a presentation for the class to demonstrate how you sorted the materials.

 Engineer It

Analyze the Life Cycle of Carbon Fibers

Carbon fiber is a strong synthetic material that has low weight, can resist chemicals, and can withstand high temperatures. It is used in products such as windmill blades, airplane brakes, and race car bodies. It is expensive to produce. Why? One reason is that the materials are made using a relatively expensive process. The process requires a large amount of energy because the starting materials must go through several steps, including heating and stretching.

23. Explain how engineers might work to improve the production or consumer use of carbon fiber.

_____

_____

_____

_____

_____

_____

 EVIDENCE NOTEBOOK
24. How could plastic bottles be recycled to make plastic that could be turned into a jacket? Record your evidence.

Continue Your Exploration

Name: _____   Date: _____

Check out the path below or go online to choose one of the other paths shown.

Careers in Engineering

- **Hands-On Labs** 👋
- **Researching Life Cycles**
- **Propose Your Own Path**

Go online to choose one of these other paths.

Materials Engineer

Materials engineers study how a material's properties are related to its structure. They learn how processing affects the material's properties. Materials engineers develop new materials with specific properties that are suited to their applications. They also develop processes to make these materials, and they test the materials' properties.

Materials engineers work on many kinds of materials in many different products, such as new materials that allow cell phones to work faster or store more information. They make materials that help to restore and protect art. They develop materials that are used inside the body to treat medical conditions. Materials engineers even help protect the environment. They can develop materials that can detect and remove toxic chemicals from water. They are also finding ways to make biodegradable plastics.

This engineer is preparing liquid glass for use in bone implant research. When hardened into foam, the bioactive glass is used as a scaffold for growing human bone.

Continue Your Exploration

1. A materials engineer is developing new materials that can withstand high-heat environments, such as rocket engines. How might understanding the chemical makeup and properties of materials help the engineer design these materials?

2. People with severe burns need their skin to heal. They often require skin grafts to cover burned areas until they heal. However, the burns can sometimes be too extensive to use the patient's own tissue for the graft. How might this need of burn patients drive materials engineers to make new materials?

3. When boats transporting oil crash or run aground, the water can become polluted with large amounts of crude oil. Because the density of oil is less than that of water, the oil will remain on the water's surface. The oil can then spread and be moved around by water movement and wind. If you were a materials engineer, how would you design a material that could contain the spill and remove as much of the oil from the water as possible?

4. **Collaborate** With a partner, discuss how materials engineers might be involved in the development of synthetic diamonds. What might drive them to want to make diamonds? How might they develop a process to make them? Create a flow chart that shows the life cycle of a synthetic diamond, from inspiration to final product.

Can You Explain It?

Name: _____   Date: _____

How can the same molecules that make up the bottles later be used to make the jacket?

EVIDENCE NOTEBOOK
Refer to the notes in your Evidence Notebook to help you construct an explanation for how the material in plastic bottles can be turned into material to make a jacket.

1. State your claim. Make sure your claim fully explains how the material in plastic bottles can be turned into material to make a jacket.

2. Summarize the evidence you have gathered to support your claim and explain your reasoning.

Checkpoints

Answer the following questions to check your understanding of the lesson.

Use the photo to answer Questions 3–4.

3. Which stages of the life cycle of the bowl happen directly before and directly after the stage shown in the photo? Select all that apply.

    A. The production stage happens immediately before.

    B. The distribution stage happens immediately before.

    C. The disposal stage happens immediately after.

    D. The obtaining resources stage happens immediately after.

4. The production of the plastic bowl is driven by the desire / need to have products to prepare food. The color of the bowl reflects the desire / need to have decorative, functional items. The use of the bowl could reflect the need / value that home cooked meals are better than fast food.

Use the photo to answer Questions 5–6.

5. What is a positive impact on society of the synthetic material being consumed in the photo?

    A. Pollution is likely reduced.

    B. Human health is likely improved.

    C. Natural resources are likely conserved.

    D. Carbon dioxide emissions are likely reduced.

6. How are engineers likely to affect the life cycle of a synthetic medicine? Select all that apply.

    A. by optimizing reaction conditions to reduce the cost of making the medicine

    B. by developing ways to package the medicine so that it cannot be opened by children

    C. by determining the price of the medicine to maximize the profit for the company

    D. by regulating the medicine so that it must be prescribed by doctors

7. Which stages of the life cycle of a new synthetic material are likely to have a positive effect on the economy by providing jobs? Select all that apply.

    A. extraction of new resources

    B. production of the material

    C. distribution of the material

    D. disposal of the material

Interactive Review

Complete this section to review the main concepts of the lesson.

Synthetic materials are developed based on consumers' needs, wants, and desires. A five-stage life cycle is one way to model all the ways in which synthetic materials and products can affect society.

A. Make a sketch to show the life cycle of a synthetic material.

Each stage of the life cycle of a material can have positive and negative effects on the environment and society.

B. Explain two positive and two negative effects that a synthetic material could have on society.

Engineers are involved in all stages of the life cycle of synthetic materials.

C. Give an example of the type of improvement an engineer could design for each stage of the life cycle of a synthetic product.

Choose one of the activities to explore how this unit connects to other topics.

Music Connection

Synthetic Materials in Musical Instruments In the past, musical instruments were made entirely out of natural materials. Advances in technology have helped manufacturers develop synthetic alternatives.

Research an instrument that can now be made in part or completely from synthetic materials. Create a multimedia presentation that combines text, sounds, and images to demonstrate the pros and cons of using each material to make that instrument.

Life Science Connection

Effects of Plastics on Animals Many animals will be exposed to one or more human-made chemicals in their lifetimes. Several of these chemicals are byproducts of plastic manufacturing, or in some cases chemicals found in plastic products.

Choose an animal that has been especially affected by the manufacture and use of plastics. Create an oral presentation of your findings to deliver to your class. Describe how society could help reduce the effects of harmful chemicals found in plastics on animals.

Computer Science Connection

E-Cycling Today, electronic products quickly become obsolete. People regularly upgrade to the newest cell phones, tablets, computers, and televisions. What happens to the outdated and discarded electronics? One option besides disposal is e-cycling, the reuse or recycling of electronic components.

Research e-cycling to understand what it is and how it works. Then research e-cycling facilities in or around your community. Create a visual display that includes electronic parts that can be recycled, the recycling process, and why e-cycling is important to your community. Present your findings to your class.

Name: _____   Date: _____

Complete this review to check your understanding of the unit.
Use the diagram to answer Questions 1–3.

1. Solar panels can be installed on the outside of buildings to supply energy using
   sunlight. What properties should the panels have? Select all that apply.

   A. easily flammable

   B. waterproof

   C. heavy

   D. durable

2. Which part of the diagram represents the
   obtaining resources stage of the material
   life cycle?

   A. wafer

   B. cell

   C. module

   D. silicon

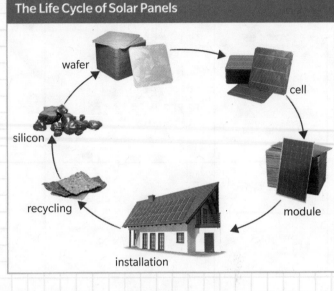

The Life Cycle of Solar Panels

wafer

cell

silicon

recycling

module

installation

3. Which stages of the material life cycle are
   shown in the diagram?

   A. obtaining resources, production, distribution, consumer use, and disposal

   B. obtaining resources, distribution, and consumer use

   C. obtaining resources, production, consumer use, and disposal

   D. obtaining resources, production, and distribution

Use the diagram to answer
Question 4.

4. Disposal of waste in landfills
   can result in which of
   the following? Select all
   that apply.

   A. overflowing waste
      in landfills

   B. pollution of airways

   C. pollution of waterways

   D. regeneration of resources

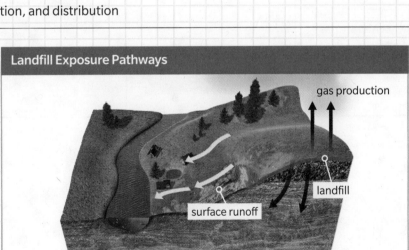

Landfill Exposure Pathways

gas production

landfill

surface runoff

5. What are some possible benefits of using a synthetic material? Select all that apply.

   A. Synthetic materials can replace all natural materials.

   B. Synthetic materials can help preserve food and are used in medicine.

   C. Synthetic materials can be less expensive alternatives to natural materials.

   D. All synthetic materials can be recycled.

6. Think about the stages of a material's life cycle when filling out this chart. Describe how these phases are related to each of the big picture concepts.

Phase	Energy and matter	Scale, proportion, and quantitiy	Real-world impacts
obtaining resources	energy is required to power the processes used to harvest the resources used to produce the material		
production			
distribution			
consumer use			
disposal			

Name: **Date:**

Use the image to answer Questions 7–10.

7. Latex, or rubber, is very water resistant, slip proof, and durable. Describe some useful everyday applications for latex.

Latex is collected from a rubber tree in Phuket Province, Thailand.

8. A special tapping knife is used to shear off a thin layer of the bark so the latex can flow into a bucket. After the latex is collected, formic acid is added to coagulate the liquid latex into a solid. What problems would arise if synthetically-produced formic acid were not added to the natural latex?

9. Describe the life cycle of rubber from its collection from a rubber tree to the disposal of a product intended for consumer use.

10. Rubber production influences the local people harvesting the rubber, the trees and environment from which it is harvested, and the land where rubber products are discarded. What are possible negative and positive effects of rubber production and disposal?

Use the diagram to answer Questions 11–13.

11. Animal skins are used to produce natural leather. To produce a leather hide, the skins are cured with salts, soaked in a lime bath, tanned, dried out, softened with oils, and heated. How does this compare to the process of making synthetic vinyl leather shown in the diagram? What portion of the vinyl life cycle does the diagram represent?

12. Synthetic leather is used to make luggage, wallets, car interiors, sofas, and shoes. What chemical and physical properties do you think synthetic leather needs to have?

13. Why might consumers prefer synthetic leather to natural leather?

14. What stages in the material life cycle occur after the last step shown in the diagram?

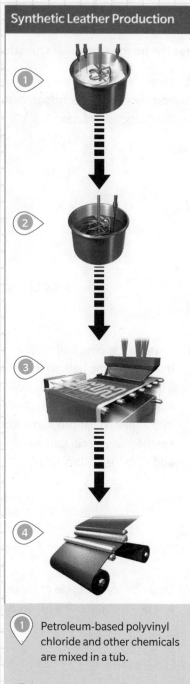

Synthetic Leather Production

1. Petroleum-based polyvinyl chloride and other chemicals are mixed in a tub.

2. Dyes are added.

3. The vinyl is poured out onto a flat surface and heat is applied to harden it.

4. Finishes are added for durability and the vinyl is formed into the final product.

Name: .   Date:

Which fencing option is best?

Imagine you are a salesperson for a fence installation company. You have meetings with three clients—a school superintendent, a suburban homeowner, and a rural homeowner—to discuss fencing options. You have been asked to identify the best fencing material for each client's needs: metal, vinyl, or wood. Provide a recommendation to each client for which type of fencing to install.

wood   metal   vinyl

Fences can be constructed from wood, metal, or vinyl.

The steps below will help guide your research and develop your recommendation.

Engineer It

1. **Define the Problem** Write a statement defining the problem you have been asked to solve. What are the criteria and constraints involved in selecting a fencing material for each client?

Engineer It

2. **Conduct Research** Research the properties and design characteristics of each material, as well as the potential benefits and drawbacks of using them. Then, research specific details regarding the life cycle of each of the three materials.

3. **Analyze Data** Evaluate each material's ability to meet the criteria and constraints for each client. Would more than one fencing material potentially meet a client's needs?

4. **Identify and Recommend a Solution** Identify the best fencing material for each client based on your research. Explain your reasoning and describe any tradeoffs that you may have considered in your decision.

5. **Communicate** Prepare a project proposal with your recommendation for each client. Your presentation should provide evidence explaining why the selected fencing material best meets the client's needs, as well as the strengths and weaknesses of each fencing material.

✓ **Self-Check**

	I clearly defined the problem and identified its criteria and constraints.	
	I researched the life cycle of each material.	
	My recommendation is based on evidence gathered from my research.	
	My recommendation is clearly communicated to the client.	

Glossary

Pronunciation Key							
Sound	Symbol	Example	Respelling	Sound	Symbol	Example	Respelling
ă	a	pat	PAT	ŏ	ah	bottle	BAHT'l
ā	ay	pay	PAY	ō	oh	toe	TOH
âr	air	care	KAIR	ô	aw	caught	KAWT
ä	ah	father	FAH•ther	ôr	ohr	roar	ROHR
är	ar	argue	AR•gyoo	oi	oy	noisy	NOYZ•ee
ch	ch	chase	CHAYS	o͞o	u	book	BUK
ĕ	e	pet	PET	o͞o	oo	boot	BOOT
ĕ (at end of a syllable)	eh	settee lessee	seh•TEE leh•SEE	ou	ow	pound	POWND
ĕr	ehr	merry	MEHR•ee	s	s	center	SEN•ter
ē	ee	beach	BEECH	sh	sh	cache	CASH
g	g	gas	GAS	ŭ	uh	flood	FLUHD
ĭ	i	pit	PIT	ûr	er	bird	BERD
ĭ (at end of a syllable)	ih	guitar	gih•TAR	z	z	xylophone	ZY•luh•fohn
ī	y eye (only for a complete syllable)	pie island	PY EYE•luhnd	z	z	bags	BAGZ
îr	ir	hear	HIR	zh	zh	decision	dih•SIZH•uhn
j	j	germ	JERM	ə	uh	around broken focus	uh•ROWND BROH•kuhn FOH•kuhs
k	k	kick	KIK	ər	er	winner	WIN•er
ng	ng	thing	THING	th	th	thin they	THIN THAY
ngk	ngk	bank	BANGK	w	w	one	WUHN
				wh	hw	whether	HWETH•er

atom (AT•uhm)
the smallest unit of an element that maintains the properties of that element (27)
átomo la unidad más pequeña de un elemento que conserva las propiedades de ese elemento

change of state (CHAYNJ UHV STAYT)
the change of a substance from one physical state to another (88)
cambio de estado el cambio de una sustancia de un estado físico a otro

chemical bond (KEM•ih•kuhl BAHND)
the attractive force that holds atoms or subunits of atoms together (43)
enlace químico fuerza atractiva que mantiene unidos a los átomos y a las subunidades de los átomos

chemical equation (KEM•ih•kuhl ih•KWAY•zhuhn)
a representation of a chemical reaction that uses symbols to show the relationship between the reactants and the products (138)
ecuación química una representación de una reacción química que usa símbolos para mostrar la relación entre los reactivos y los productos

chemical formula (KEM•ih•kuhl FOHR•myuh•luh)
a combination of chemical symbols and numbers to represent a substance (134)
fórmula química una combinación de símbolos químicos y números que se usan para representar una sustancia

chemical reaction (KEM•ih•kuhl ree•AK•shuhn)
the process by which one or more substances change to produce one or more different substances (122)
reacción química el proceso por medio del cual una o más sustancias cambian para producir una o más sustancias distintas

compound (KAHM•pownd)
a substance made up of atoms of two or more different elements joined by chemical bonds (43)
compuesto una sustancia formada por átomos de dos o más elementos diferentes unidos por enlaces químicos

crystal (KRIS•tuhl)
a solid whose atoms, ions, or molecules are arranged in a regular, repeating pattern (51)
cristal un sólido cuyos átomos, iones o moléculas están ordenados en un patrón regular y repetitivo

density (DEN•sih•tee)
the ratio of the mass of a substance to the volume of the substance (11)
densidad la relación entre la masa de una sustancia y su volumen

element (EL•uh•muhnt)
a substance that cannot be separated or broken down into simpler substances by chemical means (24)
elemento una sustancia que no se puede separar o descomponer en sustancias más simples por medio de métodos químicos

gas (GAS)
a form of matter that does not have a definite volume or shape (76)
gas un estado de la materia que no tiene volumen ni forma definidos

law of conservation of matter (LAW UHV kahn•ser•VAY•shuhn UHV MAT•er)
a law that states that matter cannot be created or destroyed in ordinary chemical and physical changes; also known as the law of conservation of mass (143)
ley de conservación de la materia ley que establece que la materia no se puede crear o destruir mediante cambios químicos y físicos ordinarios; también conocida como ley de conservación de la masa

liquid (LIK•wid)
the state of matter that has a definite volume but not a definite shape (76)
líquido el estado de la materia que tiene un volumen definido, pero no una forma definida

mass (MAS)
a measure of the amount of matter in an object (7)
masa una medida de la cantidad de materia que tiene un objeto

matter (MAT•er)
anything that has mass and takes up space (6)
materia cualquier cosa que tiene masa y ocupa un lugar en el espacio

molecule (MAHL•ih•kyool)
a group of atoms that are held together by chemical bonds; a molecule is the smallest unit of a compound that keeps all the properties of that substance (43)
molécula grupo de átomos unidos por enlaces químicos; una molécula es la unidad más pequeña de un compuesto que mantiene todas las propiedades de dicha sustancia

natural resource (NACH•uhr•uhl REE•sohrs)
any natural material that is used by humans, such as water, petroleum, minerals, forests, and animals (188)
recurso natural cualquier material natural que es utilizado por los seres humanos, como agua, petróleo, minerales, bosques y animales

periodic table (pir•ee•AHD•ik TAY•buhl)

an arrangement of the elements in order of their atomic numbers such that elements with similar properties fall in the same column, or group (30)

tabla periódica un arreglo de los elementos ordenados en función de su número atómico, de modo que los elementos que tienen propiedades similares se encuentran en la misma columna, o grupo

polymer (PAHL•uh•mer)

a large molecule formed of more than five smaller units that are usually joined in a repeating pattern (196)

polímero molécula grande formada por más de cinco unidades más pequeñas que suelen estar unidas en un patrón repetitivo

pressure (PRESH•er)

the amount of force exerted per unit area of a surface (99)

presión la cantidad de fuerza ejercida en una superficie por unidad de área

product (PRAHD•uhkt)

a substance that forms in a chemical reaction (122)

producto una sustancia que se forma en una reacción química

pure substance (PYUR SUHB•stuhns)

a sample of matter, either a single element or a single compound, that has definite chemical and physical properties (42, 186)

sustancia pura una muestra de materia, ya sea un solo elemento o un solo compuesto, que tiene propiedades químicas y físicas definidas

reactant (ree•AK•tuhnt)

a substance or molecule that participates in a chemical reaction (122)

reactivo una sustancia o molécula que participa en una reacción química

solid (SAHL•id)

the state of matter in which the volume and shape of a substance are fixed (76)

sólido el estado de la materia en el cual el volumen y la forma de una sustancia están fijos

synthetic material (sin•THET•ik muh•TIR•ee•uhl)

a material that is made by humans through a chemical process or reaction (192)

material sintético material creado por seres humanos mediante un proceso o una reacción química

thermal energy (THER•muhl EN•er•jee)

the total kinetic energy of a substance's particles (91)

energía térmica energía cinética total de las partículas de una sustancia

volume (VAHL•yoom)

the amount of space that an object takes up, or occupies (10)

volumen la cantidad de espacio que ocupa un objeto

weight (WAYT)

a measure of the gravitational force exerted on an object; its value can change with the location of the object in the universe (7)

peso una medida de la fuerza gravitacional ejercida sobre un objeto; su valor puede cambiar en función de la ubicación del objeto en el universo

Index

Note: Italic page numbers represent illustrative material, such as figures, tables, margin elements, photographs, and illustrations. Boldface page numbers represent page numbers for definitions.

C